Change Your Reality, Change Your Life

Change Your Reality, Change Your Life

Robin McKnight, M.A., L.P.C.

BEYOND
WORDS
Publishing
I N C

Beyond Words Publishing, Inc.
20827 N.W. Cornell Road, Suite 500
Hillsboro, Oregon 97124-9808
503-531-8700

Editor: Julie Steigerwaldt
Managing editor: Sarabeth Blakey
Copyeditor: David Abel
Cover design: Jerry Soga
Composition: William H. Brunson Typography Services

Printed in the United States of America
Distributed to the book trade by Publishers Group West

Library of Congress Cataloging-in-Publication Data
McKnight, Robin.
  Change your reality, change your life / Robin McKnight.
      p. cm.
  1. Self-actualization (Psychology).   I. Title.

BF637.S4M3927   2004
158.1—dc22

                                                2004009493

The corporate mission of Beyond Words Publishing, Inc.:
Inspire to Integrity

DEDICATION

To all the beautiful sparkles of light in my life.
You know who you are, and how
special you each are to me.

And to Kathy Klimpel,
thank you for all of your assistance.

CONTENTS

As a student of life, people are part of my studies. I have been trying to figure them out all my life. I question almost everything: Why do we do the crazy things that we do? What is going on inside our minds that leads us to these things? What is *really* going on?

The answers I have come up with form the book you hold in your hands. Think of it as "Reality 101," a basic course for getting to know and becoming comfortable with your reality. While everything I say is common knowledge in some field (or in many), it has never been put together in quite this way for this particular period in history. This book is about reality as we now know it.

I have based the answers contained in this book on many factors: my knowledge and study of people, my work as a professional counselor, my work as a behavior therapist, and my experiences as a daughter, student, wife, mother, friend, sister, acquaintance, employee, and colleague.

To begin, let me ask you a question: What's real in your reality? You're probably asking yourself, "What does she mean by that?" I mean exactly what the question asks—"What's real in your reality?"

As odd as it may seem, what is *real* to you may not be *real* to me. What is truth for you, may not ring true to me. And the factors that meld to create your experience of reality may be very different from the factors that meld to create mine. To quote Anaïs Nin, "We don't see things as they are; we see things as we are."

We each live in our own little world. Each of us has a body, mind, and soul that are unique and individual, and different from all other bodies, minds, and souls. While we share an outside reality (life on earth), we all exist or live in our own personal realities. This book explores both realities—our own personal experience of reality and our shared reality. It then explains the benefits of finding harmony between the two realities, and gives guidance for successfully navigating through both.

This book is divided into three parts. Part One explores your *personal reality*. It defines personal reality, and then describes in detail your role in that reality. You will learn how your body, mind, and soul can work together to accomplish your desires—or work against each other to keep you stuck. You will learn to own what is yours, and take responsibility for that; and to let go of the need to control what is not—and, by definition, can never really be—yours. It is a map of who you are—a map that you create and re-create, all the time.

In Part Two, *shared reality* is defined and discussed. I present five basic tenets of shared reality, and share techniques that you can use to successfully navigate your way through all five of these. You will learn what you can and cannot control in the external world; then you will learn how to control the controllable. Fun and easy exercises illustrate how simple it is to change aspects of this reality and create the experience you desire.

Finally, Part Three describes mental health as finding a balance and harmony between reality within and reality around—that is, congruence. Once you become aware of what is going on within and around you, you will begin to better control those factors that once upset you. You will begin to find answers to what were once only questions, and to discover new ways of coping.

This book is a thorough look at reality and how it pertains to you. This very valuable information is basic and essential, yet it is often ignored or denied. You have much more power and control over your life than you may currently believe. There is energy in your thoughts, emotions, and actions—though you may be unaware of it, the fact is, it is there! The more awareness that you have, the more control that you gain. With control comes personal power.

Join me as I take you inside your reality and explore it with you. You just might find the answer you've been looking for.

Personal Reality

1

Defining the Self

You *live in your own little world.* No one lives there but you. This space that is within and around you *is* you. It *is* your body and your mind and your soul, and the complex interaction that all of these have with the world around them. It is the whole of who you are. It is what you think, and how you feel, and what you believe, and how you react. It is the being called "you." And you are the only one just like you.

Who are you? You are the product of all that exists within you. Everything you have ever seen, known, thought, felt, or been is stored up in energy, in the space that is within and around you. All of these things bind together in some way to define you to the rest of the world. What is interesting, though, is that no two people will experience you in exactly the same way, because each of them is separate and has alternate realities on which to base their judgments. Thus everyone's perception of everyone else is unique. No two people see anything in exactly the same way.

The two organs that sustain your life are your heart and your brain. Your heart cannot function without the brain telling it to;

your brain cannot function without the blood supplied by the heart. You can't have one without the other for any extended period of time. Life is dependent on both working together.

Yet, while these two organs are totally dependent on each other—and the rest of the body dependent on them—there is an even greater factor that gives life to both. Some call this your "soul," "true self," "spirit," "God-self," or "essence." It is the energy that *is* the life within the body. It is what allows both brain and heart to function. It existed before you were born, and it moves on after you die. It is life itself. Your essence. Your gift.

The light of life exists within us all. It is the *only* common denominator in every living thing. It is the one thing that we all share. We all share this energy of life, thus we are part of and connected to all life. We are of the same fabric—the same light.

While we are totally individual and unique, we are also completely entwined with all of the other life that exists around us. While each of us exists in our own personal reality, we must also participate in a shared reality. No one can exist in a vacuum. Other life is required to support our life; we help each other to exist. In this way, we maintain connectedness. We become part of something larger, and new meaning is added to our lives. We don't feel so alone.

So, you are a soul, housed in a body, controlled by a mind, living in a world shared by other souls housed in bodies that are controlled by minds. Thus, we each have our own personal reality, within the context of a shared reality.

Being separate and also connected is not a "bad" thing. In fact, it is really the best of both worlds. We have ourselves (our ultimate confidantes and most trusted friends), and we have others (companions to walk through life with). We have a world of thoughts, impressions, and dreams in our minds, and we share a set of thoughts, impressions, and dreams with the world around us. What more could you ask for? You are given a life–complete with a body, a mind, and the ability to feel, know, and experience physical reality. You get to touch and feel and taste and smell and hold physical reality.

Seeking A Balance	
Reality Within	**Reality Around**
Internal plane	Physical plane
Freedom	Connectedness
Individuality	Love connections
Internal experience of love	Physical experience of love
Life within	Life around
You	You with another
The mind/thoughts	Voice/expression
Dreams	Physical reality
Internal reaction	Physical experience
Something all your own	Something to share

Imagine for a moment what life would be like without the body. It wouldn't be life as we know it. Imagine all that you wouldn't be able to taste or touch or hear or feel or smell. Reality would be completely different without these sensations. They are what provide us pleasure in this lifetime. They are what separate us from other beings. They are our greatest gifts in many ways.

Think of the senses and the experience of love that each can bring on a physical level. Imagine savoring a slice of your favorite dessert or embracing a loved one. Imagine walking into a room and smelling an incredibly wonderful scent, or hearing a beautiful sound. When you are *feeling* something wonderful—truly *feeling* and experiencing it—then you know love. You feel alive and whole. You become love and life for a moment. And nothing feels better than this aliveness and love. These experiences are what make life worth living.

Yet, many of us continue to be unhappy. We feel fragmented and lost. We experience an isolation that seems to come from deep within. This worries us and keeps us feeling separate and alone.

This aloneness exists only within our minds. Yes, we each have only one body and make up only one person, but this one person lives in a context of something much larger than itself. We are part of the same *one*. We are all connected, like it or not. *It can be no other way.*

The smallness is what really makes us afraid. We don't feel like we are enough by ourselves. We know on some level that we need others in order to survive, yet we don't trust that those others will be there when we need them for survival. We feel vulnerable to others' influence on our lives, so we tend to separate ourselves. We think that insulating ourselves will keep us from getting hurt.

That is just fear. No matter how separate you feel, you still have your spirit self, your essence—which is inevitably connected to the essence of everything else. You are still part of this great big world that exists for all times and for all things. You are still, and always will be, a point of light in the universe—a point of light equal to all other points of light.

You are like a star in the night sky, where each star represents a life. Every life in this universe is important and equally worthy of this gift of life. There is value in your uniqueness. You leave your own special mark on the world. You should praise your individuality. Yet, remember that every other soul is unique and special also. Being unique does not make you "better." None of us is "better" than any other. Some try harder than others. Some do "better" deeds than others or think "better" thoughts than others, but in the end, we are all equal. We all have an equal amount of life running through us. What we choose to do or not to do with that life shapes the experience that we have during this life, but each has an equal opportunity for that experience.

Personal Reality

You may think that maintaining mental health is hard, but it is actually easy. It's a matter of challenging your thoughts—and changing your mind. You have the power and the control to do this at any point. At any time, you can see things from a different perspective, or notice something that you have never seen before. You can open your mind. You can see things in a new way. You can think about something in a new way. You can create a new thought. Personal reality is what you make it. However, there are some basics that it might help you to know.

We'll begin by examining the three main aspects of your personal reality:

- *The Body*—physical sensations and reactions
- *The Mind*—what you think and perceive
- *The Soul*—what transcends you

We'll discuss each aspect of your personal reality, and teach techniques for better control of each. You will learn the interactions that your systems have with each other. You will begin to recognize the importance and value of every part of yourself. You will begin to know yourself, and take more control in making positive changes.

You are constantly fine-tuning yourself. You re-create yourself anew every moment. So, let's begin right now!

2

The Body

Your body is an amazing network of complicated systems, all working together twenty-four hours a day, seven days a week, to help keep you healthy and alive. It is absolutely incredible to begin to fathom all of the work your body does in just a single day.

Life is continuously circulating throughout the body. The heart pumps the lifeblood into the arteries, the lungs provide oxygen, and the brain is the central processing unit of the system as a whole. Everything works together. Everything has its function. Everything does its share.

Each organ, muscle, and cell is its own entity, yet each is also part of the whole body. While each has a life of its own, its life is dependent on the life of the body. The body houses our life. Our body becomes our home. It is where we live; it is how we live.

What you do with your body is your choice, and you have choices to make. While you may have limited choices in the actual physics of your body, you do have many choices every day in how you care for it. You are responsible for caring for yourself.

No one is going to do it for you (they couldn't if they wanted to). It is your body. You must own it and take responsibility for it.

You body works more harmoniously if you love, appreciate, and take care of it. Exercise, eat right, and take care of yourself. Get rest. Find a balance between activity and stillness. Know that you need both, and try not to overindulge in either. The body needs rest and recovery time—you can only push it so far. On the other hand, if all is going smoothly within your body, then it rewards you with energy and vitality and life. You can spend more time on more important and bigger things.

How the Body Works

When food is taken in through the mouth, it goes down the esophagus on its way to the stomach, where the food is processed and digested. What is needed is absorbed into the system. What is unnecessary is discarded. The body maintains balance in this way.

In your body, each organ and system does its part to contribute to your overall health. Each organ and system has a job, and every job is necessary to keep the body running smoothly. The brain and the heart are pretty much in charge and require the cooperation and assistance of all other systems in the body. An abundance of oxygen, nourishment, and life's blood keeps the body content and nurtured. When the whole body is working together, things are balanced and in harmony. There is general health and well-being.

If there is a breakdown in any system, all of the body's components are affected on some level. Once a breakdown of the overall function of the system has occurred, the body becomes weakened and is at an increased risk of illness. Once an infection finds its way in, the body has to shift from thriving mode to barely surviving mode. Almost all of the system's energy is tied up in restoring health and healing, leaving little energy for anything else, including growth and advancement.

You may have heard of psychologist Abraham Maslow's "hierarchy of needs." Maslow theorized that our needs and basic human drives exist in a hierarchy, which he represented as a triangle. Those needs at the bottom of the triangle are the most basic and necessary for survival, and include the need for nourishment, rest, safety/protection, and shelter. Only after these needs are met can higher needs be actualized, such as examining values and self-awareness. If a person's life is taken up in trying to fulfill very basic needs, greater needs can never be addressed. If you are starving, you don't much care about your moral development. If you have no place to sleep, or can't provide for your family, then your focus is most likely not going to be on your own self-actualization.

We must meet our basic needs, and find a sense of security in knowing that they are met, before we can focus on bigger things. Take a moment to reflect on where you are spending your time and energy. Your goal should be to reach a place in which the basic needs are satisfied to the point that other things—like self-improvement and personal enhancement—can become your daily focus.

The body is designed to take care of itself. You can help it or harm it by the way that you take care of it. Whole health means that all systems are working together on all levels for the good of the whole: each is a contributing share in the whole, each is rewarded with abundance and life. While each exists on its own, each assists and supports the others.

Bodily Communication: Do You Know How to Listen?

Our bodies were created to sustain life. In an effort to maintain health, there are checks and balances throughout each individual system, as well as the system as a whole. Our body tells us when something is wrong. It is up to us to hear and listen to its messages, and heed its warnings.

How does your body talk to you? In many ways. To name a few, the body talks to you through physical sensations, knee-jerk reactions, the senses, hunger, thirst, cravings, illness or dysfunction, and feelings and emotions. Let us look at these more closely.

How Your Body Talks to You

Examples

Physical sensations	Pain, tension, temperature
Knee-jerk reactions	Startle reflex, fight-or-flight response
The senses	Taste, touch, hearing, sight, smell
Hunger/thirst	Salivation, stomach rumbling
Cravings	Overwhelming desires
Illness or dysfunction	Lack of total health; lack of sleep
Feelings and emotions	Anger, sadness, joy, love

Physical Sensations

The most obvious and measurable way the body speaks to us is through *physical sensations*. When we are threatened, we break out in a sweat, or our heart races. We get short of breath, or our muscles tighten. We feel dizzy or weak, or we get revved up for immediate action. We experience pain, or a stuffy nose.

Often, we don't want to recognize these bodily signals because they cause discomfort. They indicate a threat that something is wrong, and we don't like threats or anything being wrong. We try to ignore the signals and hope they will go away. Sometimes they do. Sometimes the signals change or become more persistent. The body becomes more desperate to communicate to you that there is a problem that needs your attention. It is trying to wake you up and get you to notice.

For example, if you have a rage reaction every time someone cuts you off on the highway, you are most likely stressing out your body's systems and maintaining your energy in anger. You are feeding this anger and allowing it to grow and take over. Once you have recognized that you are doing this, you can begin to change it by finding a new way to react. While it still may be "automatic" for you to get angry quickly, you can interrupt this pattern of rage much more quickly, and turn it into something more productive and life affirming.

Knee-Jerk Reactions

Many physical reactions are programmed within the bodily systems to sustain life. The fight-or-flight reaction is an excellent example of this. When something *startles* us or we perceive it as dangerous, the body automatically reacts in a manner that either triggers flight away from the danger or provokes a stand-up-and-fight stance to face and conquer the danger. This is an automatic process; you are wired to look out for your own safety.

Other reactions are learned. We salivate when we see and smell chocolate because we have learned that we enjoy and savor it. We anticipate the taste and enjoyment we have experienced in the past while eating chocolate. Our body maintains those memories and reacts in anticipation. The same is true for thirst. The body remembers which beverages satiate thirst, and the body craves these beverages. The body seeks to repeat pleasurable experiences while minimizing negative ones.

The Senses: Sight, Hearing, Touch, Smell, and Taste

Our five senses are perhaps our greatest gifts. What we experience through our senses defines reality for us. Everything we attempt to illustrate is described best using our senses. We describe what we see and the sounds we hear. We attempt to relate how things feel. We recognize a scent or savor a taste. Our senses bring freshness and flavor to our existence, and they enhance our experience of reality. The more senses we involve in something, the more completely we experience that thing, and the more real it becomes. Make it a goal to involve all of your senses in all of the activities of your life. These are the tools for a richer life.

Exercise: On Becoming Aware

This exercise will help you become aware of your body, there where you are right now. Becoming aware of yourself is the first step toward enriching your personal experience of reality. Become aware of your thoughts and what is going on inside your mind. Become aware of any sensations you may be feeling. Become aware of your breath.

Take a deep, long, slow breath. Hold the breath for a moment, and then slowly release it. Again, take a long, deep, slow breath. Hold it for a moment, and then slowly release it. Continue to breathe deeply throughout this exercise.

Give yourself a moment to become aware of yourself.

If your eyes are open, what do you see? (Not just the objects, but the reality that exists around you.)

What do you hear going on around you? What sounds are continuous? And which ones are transient?

Can you smell anything?

Is there a taste in your mouth?

How does your body feel at this moment? Do you notice any physical sensations?

When you have taken in all of these sensations and really felt them for a while, then slowly begin to become aware of the room around you again. Take your focus from within yourself out to your surroundings.

It is that easy to tune in and pay attention to your body. Repeat this simple exercise several times a day. Simply become aware.

Hunger/Thirst

Every day in America, many people gorge themselves with food and overindulge. The body's physical sensations trigger hunger, so we seek food. We consume so quickly and so mindlessly that when the body sends out the "I'm full" response, we ignore it and continue eating. Soon the body has more food than it can digest. Indigestion, gastric reflux, bloating, and pain soon follow. We have ignored the body's natural response of feeling satisfied and full and continued to eat—most likely due to the influence of the mind and our thoughts. Meanwhile, the body suffers and has to put its energy into a massive attempt to process the overload.

Our thoughts about food strongly influence our eating behaviors. We are so concerned about waste and cost that we often eat more than we need just to keep it from going bad or being thrown away. We also want to feel like we are getting all that we pay for, so we consume huge portions just to feel like we have gotten our money's worth. While there is nothing wrong with eating what we've paid for, there is a problem with eating to the point that it makes us miserable. Overeating is a huge national problem. We must begin to learn to eat until we are full and then stop!

The key to interrupting any dysfunctional pattern is awareness. By becoming aware of your body's physical reactions, you become more self-aware. Begin to pay attention to your body's sensations and reactions, especially around food and eating. Listen to what your stomach is telling you, not what your mind is telling you. Learn to control your mind when it starts beckoning you to eat for the sheer pleasure of it. Ask your mind what it really wants—comfort, pleasure, or something to do is probably closer to the answer than actual hunger. Eat if you are hungry, and eat for your health. Do not eat for any other reason.

When you do eat, enjoy what you eat and savor the experience of eating it. Use the following guidelines at meal times.

Mindful Eating

- **Eat only when you are hungry.** Don't eat because it is time, or because you think you need to. Listen to your stomach; it will tell you when it is ready.
- **While eating, do nothing but eat.** If you are involved in several other activities while you are eating, your attention is on the other activities—not the food you are putting into your mouth. Thus, you put more and more food into your mouth. Place your full attention on the flavor, feel, and experience of your meal. Not only will you enjoy it more, you are less likely to make yourself miserable.
- **Breathe and drink between bites.** Perhaps the best mealtime advice it is to slow down the pace of your meal. Between bites, breathe, drink water, and take a moment or two to talk to whoever might be with you. Give your food some time to digest before eating more, especially toward the end of the meal.
- **Enjoy what you are eating, or stop.** It's that simple.
- **Stop eating when you are satisfied or full.** Pay attention to your abdominal area and learn your body's signals.
- **Eat small amounts, frequently, throughout the day.** Think of it as reinforcing yourself often. Just don't get carried away.
- **Better in the trash than on your hips.** Let go of guilt for not eating every morsel on your plate. Starving children aren't going to benefit from your making yourself miserable by overeating. Put less on your plate to start with, or learn other ways to share, conserve, and keep waste to a minimum.

Mindful Eating

- **Learn from your mistakes.** You are sick for three hours because you overate at dinner, yet you do it again the next day. That makes no sense. Why would you make yourself miserable? Learn to control your mind when it tells you that you need something. Listen to your body, not your mind. It is not as easy for your body to lie.
- **Know your limits.** Maintain those boundaries—in all forms of consumption.

Client Example. I had a client who was fighting her weight constantly, and because she was getting bigger, her weight was winning. After we discussed the circumstances around her weight gain, I asked her to follow this plan, and to bring her results back into therapy with her.

Action Plan

1. **Examine your intentions** and motivations for continuing a particular behavior (in this case, eating).
2. **Change your thoughts and perceptions** in some way to better serve you as a person (change your views about yourself and the reasons why you eat).
3. **Change your behavior.** Do something different. Or keep the behavior (like eating) and make it less harmful to the body (by eating healthier foods and drinking more fluids).

1. *Examine the intentions.* To help my client identify her reasons for eating, I asked her to note the reason each time that she ate for an entire week. This would show what was motivating her behavior. Every time she wanted to eat, she asked herself, "Am I really hungry, or is there some other need I am feeling right now that I am mistaking for hunger?"

2. *Change the thoughts.* The thoughts running around in her head were not healthy, and needed to be replaced with healthier thoughts and perceptions. We started with her affirming to herself numerous times a day that she was losing weight now and that she was not gaining any more.

3. *Change the behavior.* I asked her to stop eating, and start playing the piano, or writing, or doing some other activity instead. She needed to find a pleasurable replacement for eating. Eating is not a pastime, but it is pleasurable way to nourish the body.

4. *Keep the behavior but make it healthier.* If she was really hungry, and there had been a satisfactory interval of time since she'd last eaten (an hour or more), then she could have a light snack. If she just wanted to munch on something, she could crunch small ice chips, chew gum, or snack on fat-free breadsticks, popsicles, raw vegetables, or fruit. She was also to double her fluid intake.

As therapy progressed, she realized that she had been eating for many reasons other than hunger, and she began to find other ways to fulfill those needs. She also found that if it was consumption that she craved, she could consume in healthier ways. She could have all she wanted of some things, and it would not harm her in any way. We also worked on her finding pleasure in other activities. Soon she was happily involved in new hobbies and losing those unwanted pounds.

Cravings

Often your body speaks to you through cravings—sustained desires. It is important to differentiate whether the craving is of the body or of the mind.

Example: You see someone eating your favorite candy. Your mind says, "Yummy. That looks good. I want some of that candy."

And you start craving that candy. You can't stop thinking about. You know you have to have it. This is a craving of the *mind.*

The mind reminds your body over and over again that it is thinking that this candy would taste good and be pleasurable. You can acknowledge the thoughts and then dismiss them and move on to other thoughts; feed the thoughts until the candy becomes an obsession; or allow yourself a small portion just to satisfy the craving.

Example: You are working at your desk when, out of nowhere, you want milk, or something made with onions and green peppers, or something with garlic in it. No events led to this craving; you just suddenly felt that you needed or wanted a particular food. This is a craving of the *body.* What you crave is generally nutritious, and almost always contains some vitamin the body may need at this time. For example, women may crave milk or milk products during hormonal times in an effort to provide the body with the extra calcium and vitamin D that it needs. It has also been suggested that people crave chocolate, especially when depressed, because it increases serotonin levels in the brain. These are examples of how the body speaks to you and tells you what it needs. It is up to you to decipher the messages.

When you realize that you are craving something, ask yourself if any thoughts or events triggered the craving. Is there something else you are craving besides just this food or beverage? Is there something more you want—such as comfort or satisfaction? Do you really want this third piece of cake, or do you want to feel fulfilled and satisfied? Understanding it may not make the craving go away, but at least you've become aware of what you are really craving. Most likely, these things are not fulfilled by food. Instead, they come from within. You have to feel them to know them.

My advice is to satisfy the craving, so that you can stop thinking about it and move on to something else. Be careful to do everything in moderation, however. Stop after one piece of cake, not the entire cake. Savor every bite—taste it, smell it, feel it on your tongue and in your mouth. Notice the sensation of satisfaction in your body when you are finished. Be grateful for the fulfillment of your desire. Feel fulfilled. The best way to end a craving is to satisfy it. The best way to satisfy it is to recognize it. Be conscious of the experience.

Illness or Dysfunction

Your body also speaks to you through physical illness. Being tired, feeling sluggish or achy, and other physical symptoms are often the first signs that an illness is coming. Your body is slowing you down so that it can focus its energy on getting well.

Your body has amazing healing powers, but it must be allowed to use them. If you are burning the candle at both ends by not eating right or getting rest, then your body is at a great disadvantage. It is already stressed by the illness and is having to ration where it places its energy. You can help it by providing it with what it needs for healing: adequate nutrition, plenty of rest, lots of fluids, and, if possible, light physical exercise.

Sleep Suggestions

One way the body communicates dysfunction is through difficulty in sleeping—and, of course, lack of sleep just aggravates any dysfunction. The body must have rest to survive. Thus, getting adequate and restful sleep should be a priority in your life. You absolutely need it to function at your best.

Going to bed is a transition time during which we leave behind the day that we have just experienced, and say hello to the night of rest that we are about to receive. As with all transition times, it helps to have routine cues that serve as reminders to the body—in this case, that it is time to calm down and rest. The

Sleep Suggestions

following suggestions are things that you can do thirty minutes or so before you wish to go to sleep for the night. Adjust these techniques to fit your lifestyle and preferences.

- **Drink decaffeinated or herbal tea or an alternate warm beverage.** Drinking a warm beverage before bed is a wonderful transitional behavior that creates a bridge between the craziness of the day and the relaxation of the evening. As you drink the beverage, breathe in the steam from the mug and clear away the stresses of the day. Use this time to process any information overload from the day, for once you are ready to sleep, you are not allowed to think about these things anymore.
- **Read something relaxing just before bed.** As long as the material isn't energizing or fear-provoking, it is OK to read it right before bed. Reading is a great way to get your mind off of the day and onto a good night's rest.
- **Have a nighttime grooming routine.** As you do your evening grooming, make a conscious effort to wash away the day you have just had, and prepare yourself for a good night's sleep. Tell yourself that the day is done and that another one does not begin until tomorrow morning. Allow yourself to have the night to get some rest.
- **Sing yourself a lullaby.** Sing or hum yourself a comforting and relaxing tune, and see yourself getting tucked in and kissed goodnight.
- **Turn off your thoughts.** Turn off your thoughts like you would turn off a radio. Imagine a radio beside your bed, buzzing a news report of your day. Mentally reach over and turn the knob all the way until it clicks off. As you do this, tell the thoughts to stop. Turn them off, and refuse to let them turn themselves back on.
- **Say your prayers.** Use the time before bed to say your prayers, or review all of the things that you are grateful for in your life. Or, mentally tell everyone that you know goodnight, and that you love them and wish them well. Send them love, and you will feel their love for you coming back.

(Continued on next page)

Sleep Suggestions

(Continued from previous page)

- **Use guided imagery CDs.** If you still have problems sleeping after trying all of the previous suggestions, put on some headphones and listen to a bedtime guided imagery CD or tape. Find one that you like and that is specifically for use before bedtime. Listen to it as you drift off to sleep.

Action Plan:
What To Do When Your Body Is Telling You Something

Step One: *Decide to see the signals.* When the body sends you signals, be aware of them. Simply recognize the signal and acknowledge it. Don't feed it or fret over it or give it undue attention. Just acknowledge what you are feeling. For example, "I notice areas of tightness in my back." Or, "My head is stuffy, but I am otherwise comfortable."

Step Two: *Do what you can do immediately.* If you can do something to help yourself feel more comfortable (such as changing your position, stretching, or rubbing a sore spot), then do it.

Step Three: *Look for patterns.* If this is a chronic problem, think about other times when you have felt this way. Is there a pattern to the times when you remember feeling like this? What might your body be telling you? What can you do about it? Question your experience. Weigh your options.

Step Four: *Develop a plan of action.* If you determine that something can be done, decide in what order to do it. What can you do now? What can you do tomorrow? What can you do in the future? Make sure that awareness, and checking in with yourself routinely, are high on this list.

Step Five: *Implement your plan.* Put your plan into action.

Step Six: *Modify your plan as necessary.* Reevaluate continuously.

Feelings and Emotions

Your body often communicates your emotions and feelings. If your body is tense and your reactions are exaggerated, you are probably in a negative emotional state. On the other hand, if your body is relaxed, your breathing is deep, and you are able to focus on one thing at a time, you are probably in a relaxed and pleasant state of mind. Your body reacts to your emotional states. Your mind has a lot to do with your emotional states, so this will be discussed more in the next chapter. For now, suffice it to say that when your body is screaming something at you, check in with your emotions to see if they are trying to tell you something.

Learning to Relax the Body

One basic principle in body awareness is learning to relax. This is an essential ingredient in gaining control over both your mental and your physical health. The best way to learn to relax is to learn to control your breathing. First, pay attention—your breathing patterns reveal a lot about what is going on inside of you. If your breaths are quick and shallow, you are most likely not in a deep state of relaxation. On the other hand, if your breaths are very deep and slow, you are most likely not stressed out.

Exercise: Listening to the Body (and Responding)

Take a few minutes to notice how you are feeling. Become aware of your body, and the position you are in. Is there anywhere that feels uncomfortable? Describe in your mind the discomfort. Get a picture of it in your mind if one comes to you. Tight muscles might look like a rope pulled tightly and stretched. Pain may seem like a color. Accept as appropriate whatever image you get. The idea is to become aware of how you feel, and to be able to recognize this feeling the next time you notice it.

If you find that certain muscles are tight, relax them. "How?" you may ask. Just tell them to relax. Your muscles are controlled by your brain, so you can use your brain to create an image that counters whatever tension you are feeling. Breathe into the tight area as if your nostrils are at the point of pain. Untie the muscles with your imagination if they are knotted up.

Imagine the brain signals running through your body to the pain. Watch the brain signals telling the muscles to relax, and sending them the energy to do so. See the area responding. You will feel a sensation of relaxing. The tension will drain from your body, allowing peace. You will feel for a moment the incredible sensation of being relaxed.

If your brain needs to send several messages of relaxation, then allow it to do so, until you notice a difference in the level of discomfort. The longer you focus on the feeling of that area relaxing, the more relaxed it will become. Keep talking to the area as long as you need to—directing it and supporting it to heal itself. And because you are the brain, you actually have the power to help it heal. You send it that power and feel empowered yourself. Your body has an incredible capacity to heal—you have this incredible capacity. But you often interfere with this capacity. When you do not take care of yourself, you make life harder on all of your internal systems. It is like the boss overstressing his employees, and the trickle-down effect of being overworked and underpaid, with no appreciation at all.

When you are ready, become aware again of the room around you. Return your focus from within yourself to the reality around you. Know that you have with you at all times the power of your mind to affect your body.

In Conclusion

Listen to what your body is telling you. If it says that you need rest, find a way to get some decent rest. Allow yourself that rest, knowing that you must learn to take care of yourself. If you are not healthy, you simply cannot function at the same level as when you are well. If your body says it needs nourishment of a specific kind (food, drink, comfort, love, fulfillment), find a way to make this a priority—even if it is just for a minute or two a day. But most of all, begin to use the power of your mind to heal yourself. Tell yourself that you are better and know that it is true.

Your natural state is a healthy state; you have energy, and you exude light and love. Life may wear you down at times, but you have the capacity to rebound. You can create things anew. You have the power to make things better. Awareness is the first step. Become aware!

3

The Mind

Every moment of every day, thoughts are running through your head. Sometimes there are several layers of thought going on all at once. They never turn off. When you are sleeping, they become your dreams. When you are awake, they are background noise. When you are "spaced out," they may not be leading the way, but they are always there.

You can decide consciously to control your thoughts, but this takes effort. You have allowed your thoughts to run wild in your mind for so long that they do not know any better at this point. Until and unless you decide to take control of them, they will run you ragged and cause much disruption in your life. Your thoughts are like small children. If not given boundaries, they take over. They make messes and wreak havoc wherever they go. They drive you crazy with their noise and endless chatter. They don't clean up after themselves, so you are left with mess after mess to deal with. They need discipline and structure and boundaries, which only you can provide. You are the adult. You have the capacity to make the decisions. Your thoughts are awaiting guidance from you. When they don't get that, then they make their own rules and live by their own hedonistic urges.

You must shape and mold your thoughts into what you would like them to become. You must shape them wisely, though, for once they are shaped, they tend to stay that way until they are reshaped later on.

Since your thoughts are going to run twenty-four hours a day, seven days a week anyway, you might as well have some influence on what they say. In fact, it is time for you to recognize that you are the only one who can dictate what goes on inside your mind. Don't allow your thoughts to drive you crazy anymore. Train your brain.

If something is roaming around in your head, it is because you are allowing it to. You have given it access and then free reign, and then you wonder why it won't go away. You have allowed it time and space to flourish. Why should it leave now? You have fed it energy and given it life. You might not have realized this before now, but it is the truth. You have allowed that energy to take up space in your thoughts or it would not be there.

You can, however, tell unhealthy thoughts to go away, and purposely and intently change your thinking to something else. You can simply choose another thought. You can control your mind.

You're Not the Boss of Me!

When it comes down to it, you are the total boss of one single person—yourself. *You are not the boss of anyone but yourself.* You must live your own life. You cannot live anyone else's. Yours is enough. You have quite enough going on inside you. It is simply not responsible behavior to take on any more than that.

You must take care of yourself. Let your significant other take care of him or herself. Let your parents and your children live their own lives, and make their own mistakes. Guide when appropriate and always teach responsible choices, but allow each to walk their own path.

You may be entrusted with the care of others, but this does not entitle you to ownership. No one can own other living beings. They are in our lives as a gift, to experience connectedness with, and to share history with. We have each other to experience love and to take care of one another. We have each other to survive.

Molding Children, Molding Thoughts

Now, you are allowed to make and enforce rules for anyone who is under eighteen and in your care. In fact, it is your *responsibility* to make and enforce rules for these people. These people, even more so than others, need boundaries. They are looking for the definitions in life, and you are teaching them. Be aware of what you are teaching them.

Boundaries help everyone and hurt no one. Being aware of your own boundaries is part of being mentally healthy. Boundaries help define who you are; they communicate to the world, on some basic unspoken level, what you expect. When you have clear boundaries and are confident about them, people respond to that and respect them.

Being clear about your boundaries, especially with your children, is vital to being your own person. Create and define your boundaries by deciding what you will and will not allow in your life, and then enforcing this. Do not allow people—your children or others—to treat you in unacceptable ways. Develop a plan that will keep it from happening, or come up with a plan that addresses it directly the next time it does occur. Decide that you mean business, and then mean business. You may not be able to *make* anyone do what you say, but you can strongly influence certain behaviors.

A common mistake among parents is not maintaining boundaries. They threaten and yell and scream, but they don't always follow through. If you follow through, your children know you aren't kidding. If you give in, they will learn to push further. It may sound cold and harsh, but it is true. Your children may thank you and appreciate the second chance, but they may also take advantage of it without even consciously knowing it. It is better not to set boundaries than to give in and allow your children to cross the ones you set. Examine closely the rules that you create, and why you create them. Once you have logically thought them through and finalized them, enforce them. You must stand your ground and mean what you say.

It is never too early to teach your children to take responsibility for their actions—and it is never too late. In fact, it is the most responsible thing that you can do for yourself and your children. When you are responsible for your thoughts, behaviors, actions, and emotions, you are taking responsibility for your life. This is a valuable lesson for anyone.

Whether or not you have children, this advice may help you in controlling your own mind. It is useful to think of your thoughts as children that need to be molded and shaped. Discipline is essential while training your thoughts. Boundaries, even within your own mind, are good to examine. What you find on the outside is generally reflected somewhere within.

Thoughts Lead to Emotions

Have you ever wondered what led you to feel or experience a particular emotion? If you think it was a circumstance, think again. Circumstances themselves are neutral and have no emotional attachment assigned to them. We give them emotion by what we think about them.

Take, for example, the circumstance of losing a job. Most people would think that this circumstance is a sad and depressing event that might lead to many other bad circumstances in the future. Yet, what if you hated that job, and the only way you could get another job was to lose this one first? Or what if that job was dangerous, or negatively affecting your health? Or what if the people you worked with were all negative and depressing, and you really needed to get away from that? If any of these circumstances were present, losing the job might not be so bad. It's all a matter of perspective. It all depends on who is experiencing the circumstance, and what they bring to the experience.

We assign value and emotion to things and events. The things and events are neutral in themselves, but we give them value and emotion by the ways in which we perceive them, and based on whether we want them in our lives. We give them power, or take it away.

A piece of furniture is simply a piece of furniture. It is neither good nor bad, ugly nor pretty. It is just wood and upholstery and other material. We give it value and worth based on our perception of the form of this material. To one person, this may be the most beautiful piece in the world. To another, it may be the most awful. The piece doesn't change between evaluations. Only the perception is different.

So what affects that perception, and defines the thing for a person? Their mind. What you think, feel, perceive, or reason about something becomes what that thing means to you. That is how your mind perceives it. That is what becomes "real" to you.

What is so fascinating, though, and what you probably don't recognize just yet, is your incredible capacity to alter these perceptions at will. If you don't like something, but you want to like it, all you have to do is change your mind about it, and suddenly it is not so bad.

For example, imagine that your husband wears an awful shirt that you cannot stand. You think the shirt is old and ragged and ready for the trash. He, on the other hand, loves this shirt and wants to keep it forever. He is emotionally attached to it and feels that it brings him luck.

Because you are trying to improve your thoughts and the atmosphere in your mind, you decide that you would like to see the value in this shirt as much as he does. So, you consciously decide to change your thinking about the shirt. You stop paying attention to how it looks and you begin to notice how the shirt affects your husband. You see him smile when he is wearing it. You notice how he takes care of it differently than some of his other clothes. You notice subtle changes in his attitude when he is around this shirt. You begin to appreciate this shirt and the happiness and comfort it provides to your loved one. You recognize the reasons that it is important to him, and instead of being threatened by that, you appreciate that. You now value the shirt simply because he does, or because it makes him feel good and you enjoy seeing him feel good.

At first, it may feel like you are pretending to like the shirt. This is OK. You have to pretend at first, to try on the new emotion and make sure that you like it. You pretend that you like it and think newer, more positive thoughts related to it. You like the way this feels better than your previous animosity, so you let the old emotions go and decide to stick with the newer ones. You just choose another path.

Sometimes it may be difficult to change your perceptions to be positive, so you settle for changing your thoughts to be neutral. For example, you have pretended to like the shirt, you have seen how your husband loves the shirt and how it makes him feel, yet you still hate the shirt. If you can't make yourself like it, then perhaps you can find a neutral state. You decide that you won't let it bother you anymore. You decide that it is his shirt and his body and if he wants to look silly in it, then that is his decision. You allow him to own it—since it is his to own and not yours—and let it go at that.

So, what can you change within your mind?

- *Your thoughts.* Think something different—evolve a thought into something more positive and life affirming.
- *Your perceptions.* See it from another point of view.
- *Your feelings.* Gradually change from negative to neutral to positive.
- *Your reasoning.* Find a new line of reasoning.

You can change any of these, at any time, by the sheer will to do so. It is all in your mind. You have complete control over it. If you don't like how you feel about something, find another way to perceive it that will be more comfortable.

Your thoughts create your moods and emotions. You feel an emotion, but that feeling is created by a set of thoughts and beliefs and perceptions that you have about something. If you love Elvis and he visits you in a dream, that would be much more meaningful than if someone who didn't love Elvis (or even thought that Elvis was kind of creepy) had the same dream. The symbol—Elvis—will have many different interpretations and meanings—and thus feelings associated with these different interpretations and meanings—depending on the dreamer. You define the symbols in your life by the thoughts, beliefs, and perceptions that you have about them. Those same thoughts, beliefs, and perceptions influence your moods and emotions.

The Power of the Mind

Your mind has incredible powers. Science and medicine haven't even begun to scratch the surface in understanding how much power the mind and brain really have. We know that we only use a small portion of our brain's capacity. What would happen if, over time, we began to use more? Think about that. What is preventing us from waking up those sleeping areas of the brain? And what is lying asleep in those areas? Healing capacities of the mind? Additional senses and perceptions? More areas of intelligence? No one knows. All we really know is that the mind is capable of incredible feats, and that its potential is much greater than we give it credit for.

What if the evolution of our species lies in our minds? What if our evolution is to expand our minds and use more of our brains? If this is the case, then it would be good to get a head start and begin using and controlling what we have right now.

Using Cognitive-Behavioral Therapy to Your Advantage

Most people have no idea how much control they have over their bodies, minds, emotions, and reactions. They are so stuck in a stimulus-response cycle that they never question why they are responding in these set ways. This is where cognitive-behavioral therapy comes in handy. Cognitive-behavioral therapy challenges you to examine your thinking and modify it if it is maladaptive. Cognitive-behavioral therapy works because you not only decide that you are going to change, but you also extend that decision into action. How does it work? Let me show you.

1. *Monitor your thoughts.* The first step in changing your thinking is to recognize what it is that you are thinking right now. Choose several times per day to check in with yourself, and ask yourself what is going on inside your mind. A simple example would be to ask yourself what you are thinking every time you use the restroom throughout the day. You can later expand this to every time you eat, or when you are driving—any time that you have a moment to go within, and ask yourself what is going on inside.

2. *Question your thoughts.* The next step in the process is to question your thoughts. What did you really mean by that? Why do you feel that way? How does a certain person affect you so easily? The questions can be endless. Often when you answer one question, a new one appears. One answer leads to another and another. Questioning your thoughts and motivations makes you more aware of yourself and what is going on inside your head.

3. *Notice patterns.* After you have monitored your thoughts for a couple of days, you will most likely start to notice patterns in your thinking. You may find one or two areas in your life that seem to come up more frequently in your thoughts than others. A big area for many people is finances. Other major areas of concern may be relationships or work issues. Noticing your thought patterns helps you to prioritize what you are going to work on first. It is also important to notice not just the topic that keeps repeating, but also the way it keeps repeating itself.

4. *Analyze yourself.* Once you have recognized patterns in your thinking and you have begun to question those thoughts, you have entered the realm of self-analysis. Self-analysis is any activity in which you are consciously aware of what you are doing, thinking, and feeling. A good way to practice this is to have brief counseling sessions with yourself (I will teach you how to do this later in the book). For now, it is enough to know that you have the capacity to question yourself, and that this is good for you (as long as you don't take it to an obsessive extreme).

5. *Help yourself.* Perhaps the most effective way that you can help yourself is to change your thinking toward more positive and life-affirming thoughts. You can do this in many ways. One easy way is to change the language of your thoughts to *present-tense positive*. Instead of saying, "I hope

to have enough money to make it this month," say "I have enough. Everything is OK." Statements are made in the present tense and are positive (or at least neutral) in content. The thought becomes uplifting, encouraging, and supportive. It becomes a mentally constructive thought.

Let's take a look at an example of the above points in action. You have been monitoring your thoughts for a few days, and you have noticed a pattern of thoughts about your relationship with your husband of seven years. The repeated thoughts include that you are not happy, that you are uncomfortable, that he seems distracted, and that nothing seems to go right anymore when you are together. What does that means to you? You find out by questioning these thoughts and your reactions to your husband. Let's say that he comes home from work and is distant and quiet. You notice yourself thinking that he is different and you wonder what might be going on in his mind. You may make up stories in your mind: that he is having an affair, or that he doesn't love you anymore. The longer you let this go between you, the more stories you make up. Making up stories will be discussed later, but for now, it is important to (1) recognize that you are making them up, and (2) begin to examine the stories to see if they have themes. The theme in these stories is self-worth. So the real issue here is not that *he* is unhappy, but that *you* are unhappy. You are the one with the issues of self-worth. You are the one making up the stories, and you are the one trying to figure it all out. Remember—you can only own what is yours. To fix any problem, you must determine what your role in the problem is. In this problem, you can say, "My role is to examine my issues of worth and how they might be affecting my marriage." You take responsibility for your part and only your part. You cannot own his problems. You don't want them, and you can't handle them for him anyway. You may ask, "But, hey, what if he is having an affair?" Well, that may come out later, but for now, you can only be responsible for yourself—and your part in things. What is going on inside you that makes you think things are different? Isn't it possible that he just had a bad day and is not thinking about you and your needs right now? It's best not to guess what other people are thinking, because it's impossible to know. Just deal with your issues and let others deal with their own. If they need your help, they will ask.

Pitfalls in Thinking

Pitfalls in thinking occur when your thinking goes awry. These maladaptive thought patterns occur commonly in today's society. We make up stories without knowing any facts. We exaggerate the truth. We jump to conclusions, take things personally, and see things as all good or all bad. The fact that these dysfunctional patterns are common does not make them good. Avoid these pitfalls. These thought patterns lead to disharmony and disruption. You may get a brief "energy high" from them, but it is short lived. They do far more damage than good in the long run.

Making Up Stories

At some point or other, we are all guilty of creating a story out of nothing, and feeding it way too much life. We take a two-second observation and turn it into an all-day mental drama. Something happens and we replay it in our minds over and over, altering it just a tad with each repetition. The story starts out small and semirational, but each successive version gets a little more elaborate. Pretty soon, you have a full-blown conspiracy theory. For example, say someone at work who usually says hello to you walks past you without speaking one morning. You have several choices at this point. You can assume that she has a lot on her mind this morning, or you can begin to obsess over a hundred different things you might have done to make her mad at you. The more you think about and obsess over it, the bigger this becomes in your mind. Pretty soon, you are convinced that she hates you now and is spreading rumors about you behind your back. Meanwhile, this person was just in her own little world of thoughts this morning and never even saw you. She has no idea that you are upset.

Mind Reading

Mind reading occurs when you guess what someone else is thinking. Don't pretend to know what others are thinking. If you have to know what someone is thinking, ask them. Don't guess. Guessing can get you in trouble, and it takes up too much mental time. Don't make up stories. Get the facts or let it go, but don't let it drive you crazy.

While it is not good to read other people's minds, it can be helpful at times to put yourself in someone else's shoes. This is a good empathy exercise. Ask yourself, "If I were this person, what would I think in this situation?" You must realize, though, that whatever answer you come up with is *your* answer—not theirs. You are not mind reading in this instance; you are doing an empathy exercise and trying to see things from another perspective. This is much more mentally healthy than making up stories or mind reading.

Jumping to Conclusions

At one time or another, we have all jumped to conclusions that may or may not have been accurate. This practice becomes mentally unhealthy when the conclusions are repeatedly negative, dark, or catastrophic. For example, your teenage son is out with his friends and isn't home exactly at curfew. You immediately jump to the conclusion that he must be dead or in jail. You start running through your mind all of the terrible scenarios that might have happened. You start wondering if you should call the hospitals and jails. With each passing minute, the stories in your head get bigger and bigger. Your son drives up five minutes later. He was having such a good time, he just lost track of the time. He apologizes, promises never to do it again, and heads for bed. You wasted a lot of energy.

Exaggeration

Have you ever thought, "The whole world is mad at me," "Everything is terrible!" or "This is really, really bad."? At one time or another, we are all guilty of exaggeration. But you can take it to an extreme. You can get so caught up in it that you alter your perception of reality toward this new memory that you just made up. You actually make it bigger in your mind. You carry this as emotional baggage, for it keeps you company on the cold nights. Try not to exaggerate too much. It just makes whatever you are exaggerating more real to you, and you really don't want to give that any more energy than necessary.

Personalization

This is what you are doing when you take any circumstance in the environment and internalize it, giving it significant meaning just for yourself. Remember that there are people other than you who are experiencing the same circumstances that you are. For example, let's say it rains on a day when you have plans to be outside. Instead of just blowing it off as something that wasn't supposed to happen, you obsess over how this inconveniences you. You develop a conspiracy theory that the weather gods are out to get you and that no one wants you to have fun anymore. Try not to take things so personally. Unfortunate things happen. Some things are beyond your control.

All-or-Nothing/Black-or-White Thinking

A common fallacy is thinking in terms of "all or nothing." "You are either totally devoted to me, or you don't love me at all." What an ultimatum! No matter which one you choose, you are wrong. Extremes are just that—extreme. Everything does not have to be totally good or totally bad, totally this or totally that. Try not to think in extremes. Between black and white, there is quite a bit of gray. When possible, think more toward the middle. Consider the possibility of common ground.

Your Thoughts Create the Reality You Experience

Because they constantly run through your mind, your thoughts mold your emotions and reactions by their repetition. They create the reality that you experience by defining that reality for you.

If you have a belief, you seek out things to reinforce your belief. For example, say you think the world is going to hell in a handbasket. You are convinced that everything that happens is catastrophic, and that we are destined to ruin ourselves and our planet any day now. Chances are, if you believe this, you will seek verification everywhere you go. You hear stories on the news that are sad, and it validates your belief. Everything is awful, and there is nothing anyone can ever do to make it any better. This becomes reality for you.

Now, say your neighbor, who lives basically the same kind of life that you do, thinks the world is a beautiful and special place and that people are basically good. She sees beauty and grace in everything. Chances are, she also seeks validation in her experiences. She hears of some group doing something wonderful for the environment, and she is further convinced of her beliefs. She hears of how many people came to help after a tragedy, and again her beliefs are validated.

Neither of you is "wrong" or "right;" you just have different views of things. One of you is focused on the negative side of things, while the other looks for the positive. We all seek validation for our beliefs. This is natural behavior. What you think about, you seem more to notice around you. If you are focused on all that is bad, you are going to find more and more examples of things that are bad. If you are looking for what is good, you will find more and more examples of good.

Because what you think about becomes real to you, the first step to changing your reality is to pay attention to your thoughts. You can learn to use both your emotions and your thoughts wisely.

Client Example. A client was going through an unexpected divorce, and was having a very difficult time dealing with her perceptions and changing her thoughts. I couldn't help her with her circumstances (that is not my place), so I tried to get her to be open to the possibility that something positive might come out of them.

Instead of asking her what was wrong, I asked her if there was anything right about the situation. Did anything that happened help someone? After considering it for a while, she said that she was proud of her soon-to-be-ex-husband for maintaining such an interest in their son. She felt pretty sure that he would do all that he could to keep their little one safe, and he was trying to be a good father. She was just sad because that was all she wanted when they were married—to have a little help. Now she has the help but not her husband.

She eventually changed the focus of her perceptions, away from him leaving and toward him taking responsibility for his behaviors, and having a free babysitter. It wasn't exactly what she had asked for, but it is what she got, so she made the best of the situation.

Creating New Thoughts

Before you can think new, positive thoughts, it is helpful to remove the old thoughts that may be weighing you down. Here are some removal and clearing techniques, visualization exercises aimed at helping you clear your mind. Find one that you particularly like, and use it anytime you want to clear your mind quickly and effortlessly.

As you read, imagine the scenario in your mind. See it and feel it happening. Know that what you are doing is effective.

- *Erase the board.* See your thoughts, images, and experiences written on a board (the board can be anything you imagine—a chalk board, a dry marker board, a slate). You would like to see new thoughts here, but at this moment there is no room. You need to make room for the new thoughts. Take a large eraser or cloth and wipe the board clean. When you are finished, the board is perfectly clean. Carefully and wisely consider what you might place on the board next.
- *Sweep it out the door.* The floor (your mind) is dirty and cluttered and needs to be cleared and aired out. You open the doors and windows and sweep out the dirt. You love your shiny new clean floors. Enjoy your clean space.
- *Pack and move.* To get rid of individual thoughts or thought patterns, have a moving day in your mind. Box up and move out all unwanted clutter. Take out a load of guilt and

a box of shame. Get rid of it all. You do not need it taking up your valuable space anymore. One by one, remove all unwanted thoughts. Put them on a truck going to the dump, and enjoy them being out of your house.

- *Clean the mirror.* Imagine that your mind is like a dirty mirror—all smudged with dark grease. As you begin to clean the mirror, the smudges get worse and smear around, but you are diligent and continue, using one rag or paper towel after another, until all the grease comes off easily. As you finally clear the mirror of the dirt, you catch your reflection in the glass. Your thoughts are clear and centered on this image. You see yourself anew. You recognize that at this moment in time you can start over again, and you do. Your thoughts are refreshed in the clear vision you have in front of you.

- *Become a revolving door.* Imagine a pole of light going through the center of your mind—like the pole in the center of a revolving door. The door revolves all the way around the pole. The pole is the exact center of your mind. As you focus, you notice the doors revolving slowly around the pole. As you gently sweep them around your mind, you clear out all the old thoughts and gently push them out the door. The old and ugly is revolved out, and the new and pretty is allowed in.

- *Bathe it in fire.* To release angry or pent-up feelings, imagine burning them in a blazing and transforming fire. See yourself in front of a raging fire. One at a time, imagine each thought that you would like to release written on a piece of paper. Take this paper and throw it into the fire. As the fire burns the paper, your thoughts are released and freed. It is OK to burn these images and words. You do not need them anymore. They no longer serve you. You have taken what you can from them, and now it is time for them to go.

- *Think light.* Cleanse your thoughts with pure light. Bathe your mind in a glow of light, and allow the light to transform and transcend all that you think and feel. Anytime you feel darkness, call upon the light. A request for light is never denied.

Positive Self-Talk

Once you have cleared your mind of all the dark images and thoughts, you have the option of replacing them with newer and brighter ways of thinking. The circumstances do not have to change for your view of them to change.

Positive self-talk is just exactly what it sounds like. You change the chatter in your mind from negative to neutral or positive thoughts. As you are learning to do this, it is important to keep a few things in mind:

1. *Keep self-talk in the present tense.* What is in the past is behind you, what is in the future is ahead of you. You are listening to yourself now in the present. Talk to yourself about now—in the present tense.

2. *Refocus negative thinking toward something more neutral or positive.* Change "I can't do this" to "This is difficult, but I am trying. I am learning what I can. I may need to get help, but I am working on making this better."

3. *Keep a journal for your new thoughts.* If you have trouble redirecting thoughts in your mind, writing them down in a journal is a wonderful exercise in focus. When you write, you can only write one thought at a time—even when you are thinking three or four. The act of journaling helps you to focus your thoughts and create them consciously as you go. This is a wonderful and convenient tool that you can use almost anywhere. Do this daily for maximum benefit.

4. *Believe in yourself.* You have an incredible capacity to change your life and thoughts for the better. But you must believe that you can do it. Tell yourself that you are in control. Remind yourself that everything is OK.

5. *Get creative.* The more creative you are with your images and positive thoughts, the more open you are to making them even better. In your imagination, there are no limits. You can paint any picture that you desire.

4

The Soul

What is the soul? It is the essence of a person, the spark that each of us possesses, and that animates us and gives us life beyond simple physiology. The soul is the life that transcends the physical body. It is the energy that gives life meaning.

We each have a soul or we wouldn't be alive. We all get only one soul, and all souls are equal. Each soul is a spark of God that has animated a physical body and caused life within that physical vessel. We are all made of the same material. In essence, we are all the same thing. We may look and act and sound different, for we all inhabit our own physical vessel, but the same light shines within us all.

So, we are really not all that different after all. Each of us has one soul, living in one body, controlled by one mind. We all have the same essence. We all love our children, our parents. Each of us has a set of people around us who we consider family (whether or not they are actually related to us), and we are generally willing to protect those people in any way that we can. We all have concerns about money and survival, no matter how rich or poor we are. Each of us strives to have a comfortable existence. Each of us loves and is loved by others, or at least desires to love and be loved by others. We all want the best for ourselves and for the ones whom we love. Our beliefs, our values may be expressed in different ways, but they are pretty much the same beliefs and values underneath.

Even our religious beliefs are more similar than we may think. In most religions, there is a power greater than all others—the Creator—even though we call him/her/it different names, and praise him/her/it in different ways. There is good and bad, and everything in between. Choose light over darkness. And be thankful for all that you have. Love, loyalty, faith, truth, honor: these are all basic ideals of various religions. We all believe and want the same thing.

Once we recognize that we are not so different, it becomes easier to accept others who may look different from us, or who have customs that are different from ours. Instead of seeing them as strange and different, we can begin to see them as fellow human beings—or better yet, fellow souls. Once we accept the fact that underneath we are all the same, we can begin to celebrate the sameness within us instead of hurting each other over our differences.

Soul and Spirit

Your soul lives beyond the words, thoughts, and feelings in the mind. It reaches beyond the physical limitations of the body. It is the transcendent part of your self that is always connected with all others. It is the part of you that reaches out beyond you and touches the lives that you come in contact with. It is the part of you that reaches out to your loved ones in need. It is the part of you that knows more than is being said.

The soul reminds us of what is important in life. It exudes the qualities that transcend our physical experience, and that add beauty and harmony to our lives. As you realize your capacity to guide and shape your life, as you become one with your soul, your life becomes higher and brighter. You begin to see things from a new and higher perspective. You begin to connect to a higher and finer frequency of light and love.

You have the capacity to allow the wisdom and beauty of your soul to shine through you in every moment. You may not be quiet and still enough to hear the musings of your soul. You may ignore your soul's light by simply never noticing it. You may neglect these higher experiences in life, because you are so busy with the minor details of life that the purpose and fulfillment of life passes you by. Time continues to pass, no matter how you perceive it. Only you can add richness and experience to that time by finding beauty and peace within it.

Qualities of the Soul

Certain qualities, the essences of certain emotions, are often connected with our soul. To experience these emotions is to know them. To savor life, experience as many of them as possible, as often as possible.

Patience. Patience is kind and gentle. It allows life to happen at its own pace. It makes no demands and issues no ultimatums. It quietly encourages and softly allows the energy of life to flow.

Joy. Joy celebrates life. It warms the heart and gives the skin a healthy glow of sunshine. Joy invites you to smile and your heart to sing. It gives you permission to jump up and down and hug anyone in your presence. Joy brings happiness and celebration to life.

Love. Love cherishes life and the people and things in it. Love appreciates. It recognizes the value in relationship and the importance of connections in our lives. Love seeks companionship and knows how to share. It bonds and securely connects hearts to one another. Love knows no judgment, feels no remorse, and knows no boundaries. Love has a life of its own. It lives on long after a physical life has ended.

Beauty. Beauty is found in the soul, not in the physical body. It radiates. It exudes grace and kindness. It knows love and patience. It is not boastful or proud. It holds no grudges and feels no fear. It is soft and shining.

Wisdom. Wisdom is the all-knowing teacher who stands back and observes, who takes careful consideration before any action, and who listens patiently and completely. It doesn't preach or get overly involved. It knows the difference between what is good for the soul and what is not. Wisdom never ridicules or shames. It is able to see things from a larger and wider perspective.

Kindness. Kindness is unconditional giving and grateful receiving. It is caring and sharing and connecting. It is respectful and knowing. Kindness is expressed in a smile, in a gentle touch, in a soft kiss. Kindness is found in the eyes, heard with the heart, and felt on many levels.

Purity. Purity is untainted love and light. It is sheer beauty and joy mixed with hope and kindness. It knows no darkness. It is pure light. It is the unspoiled essence of any emotion or thing. It is something in its simplest and purest form. It is the most God-like of all, for it is pure God.

Light. Light is an energy that shines life. Light dispels the darkness. It enables growth and inspires beauty. It infuses with life. It creates. It encourages movement upward, and shines unconditionally on all. Light is not prejudiced or choosy.

Security. Security is a feeling of groundedness and a knowing that everything is going to be OK. It is the feeling of safety and warmth and comfort. It is faith.

Gratitude. Gratitude appreciates. It wants nothing. It has all it needs. Gratitude recognizes the value in all that it has, and is thankful. It surpasses survival and celebrates with joy.

Peace. Peace is quiet, still, and calm. It invokes comfort and induces relaxation. It smoothes away the troubling thoughts and replaces them with soft and gentle ones.

Harmony. Harmony is balance. It is found in peaceful connections. It loves equilibrium and relativity.

Fulfillment. Fulfillment is total satisfaction. It needs nothing else. It is content and satiated. It can just allow itself to enjoy being fulfilled.

Communication with Your Soul

Your soul speaks to you continuously, but you sometimes miss its messages due to all the chaos in your mind. The mind has a tendency to block out the soul's words and feelings when it feels threatened in any way by the soul's loving and peaceful nature. Your mind controls your ego and your personality. Sometimes, your personality does not want the peaceful wisdom of the soul to shine through. Sometimes you feed on the insecurities and intense emotions of your mind. You become trapped in their seduction. You can overrule your mind, though—you can do it with your heart, and you can do it with your soul.

The best way to learn to hear what the soul has to say is to turn inward and listen. When you quiet the chatter of the mind and dismiss the leanings of the ego, you allow a quiet space to manifest. In these moments of quiet and stillness, the soul is able to communicate and be heard.

To do this, quiet your mind and find the space that lies between your thoughts. You may only be able to keep this space quiet for a few seconds at first, but any stillness is good for the soul.

As you are learning to really listen to your body and to your soul, it may be easier to start with small intervals of time—a few moments here and a few minutes there. These times can be convenient and unplanned. If you find yourself waiting somewhere, take a few moments to stop and quiet your mind. If you find yourself obsessing over something, you can simply decide that you have had enough of that for a few minutes, and allow yourself a ten-minute "time out" from your problem.

Practice being able to totally still your mind. If you absolutely cannot keep your mind totally quiet, then purposely direct your thoughts to something higher and finer. Repeat a mantra in your mind—like "peace" or "love"—and then allow that feeling to consume you. Use prayer as an option for this time and space. As with affirmations, prayer is most healthy when it is in the present tense and given from a grateful place; begging prayers are not appropriate. Thankful prayers are much more adaptive. Whatever technique you choose, the goal is the same—to allow yourself a moment of peace and quiet. Following are some additional tips.

Breathe

Learning to control your breathing is one of the most important things you can do for your mental and physical health. Your breath is vital to life, and when it is controlled, it can allow you to change your moods and emotions fairly easily. A deep and cleansing breath can wipe away a lot of frustration. A long, healing breath can cleanse the body, mind, and soul.

Close your eyes and take in a very deep, slow, healing breath. Hold the air in your lungs for a moment and feel life fill your body. Exhale through your mouth, and as you let all the air out, feel the old thoughts and emotions leaving. After the old breath departs, breathe in a new breath to fill yourself. Allow this breath to cleanse your lungs. When you are ready, release what is not needed back into the air to be recycled yet again. Follow your breath in and out until you are ready to pay attention to something else. Use your breath to relax and focus in any situation.

Meditate

There are many types of meditation. In fact, there are hundreds of books devoted to them. If you don't already meditate, I encourage to explore different methods until you find one that works well for you. Use the techniques in this book—guided imagery techniques and quiet moment meditations—as a starting point.

Exercise, or Practice Yoga

Yoga is a form of exercise that focuses on breathing and stretching. It cleanses, relaxes, energizes, and tones the body. Yoga is an excellent way to combine several mentally healthy exercises at once. While doing yoga, you are working with your breath, your muscle tone, your thoughts, and your balance. You bring your mind and body into harmony. Doing yoga regularly, especially first thing in the morning, can be a very good way to ground yourself and set your intentions for the day.

If yoga is not for you, any form of exercise is good for your body, mind, and soul. No matter what kind of exercise you choose, make sure to breathe deeply throughout it and focus your mind. The focus combined with deep, steady breathing will invite and allow the soul to awaken and speak.

Give and Share

Perhaps the truest expression of your soul is found in the act of giving and sharing. The energy of giving is very flowing. When you give and share of yourself, you flow with this energy and become one with it.

A good way to give and share more of yourself is by examining the "stuff" in your life. We often do not realize all that we have in our lives. No matter how rich or poor, the average person wants more and more. This seems to be natural in our culture, and even expected. The media tells us what to want and we buy it. Why? Because we like to buy and have things. When we have too many things and no space to put it all, then we want bigger houses or more storage to accommodate all our stuff. But quantity of stuff does not equal quality of life.

It's important to value what you currently have. If you don't have time for or enjoy all that you have now, then don't get anything else for a while. Even better, consider sharing what you have. If you don't need something in your life, if it is just there taking up space, you could give it to someone else who might really use it and appreciate it. There are plenty of people in need. If you make something available for use in the world, the world will usually find a way to use it. But you have to allow it to be used. If you have it sitting in storage or idle for extended periods of time, you might ask yourself why it is still taking up space when it could be put to good use to help someone. Chances are that if you leave it in storage long enough, it won't even be of use to anyone, and it will just become part of the trash problem on this planet.

Take a look at the waste in your life. If you know deep down that you are not going to use something, consider giving it to a friend or family member. If they can't use it, try Goodwill, Salvation Army, or another donation center in your area. Getting rid of what you don't need benefits others, is a tax write-off for you, and clears space in your garage or closet . . . not to mention your life!

Things come and go from your life as you need them. If there is a purpose they can serve that will keep you on your path to your higher good, they will find you. And when they have served their purpose, they easily take leave from your life. Trust this process by not hanging on tightly to material possessions. Allow yourself to continue to give and share.

Receive with Grace

Your soul is not only able to give freely, it is able to receive freely. While you may be comfortable in giving, you may not be so good at gracious receiving. You may not even acknowledge the gifts that you receive, or even be able to receive them. You may not feel worthy of the gifts that life brings you. But you must realize that life would not send you a gift if you weren't worthy of receiving it.

It is good to receive. No matter what your mother—or anyone else—might have told you, it is OK to take things that are freely and openly given to you. If the intentions are good, you will know, and you can trust that it is OK to accept it. It may be just what you need at this time in your life.

If you think about it, I am sure that you can remember a time when something came into your life at the perfect moment, right when you needed it the most. This happens every day; you just don't always recognize it. When you recognize that something has come into your life for a reason, it becomes much easier to accept it. You can always get rid of it later if you no longer need it. In fact, it is a part of life that it will leave at some point.

When it is time to receive in your life, be happy and appreciate that someone was kind enough to share with you. Don't question your worth or your value. Know that they would not have given it if they did not want to. Accept it, give thanks for it, and then use it to add light to your life in some way.

What Is Really Important: Connections

The only thing we take with us when we leave this place is our soul, but who we are while we're here is molded and created by the people around us. Your relationships affect the quality of your life more than anything else. For better or for worse, these people are the most important factor in your happiness. They are the group with whom you travel through time: your family members, your long-term friends, your kids, your parents, your long-term coworkers. These are also the people who help you define your version of reality. And your relationships with them are the most significant "stuff" that you have.

Client Example. A client was working on improving his relationships with his significant others. Over the course of several years that he spent making money, he lost sight of those whom he really loved. His marriage was on the rocks, his kids seemed to be pulling further away, and he hadn't spoken to his relatives in a long time. He recognized the need to improve his personal relationships, but he had no idea how to do it. The following is the very basic plan for therapy that emerged.

Goal: To improve interpersonal relationships.

Expected outcomes (set by the client): Spending more quality time with significant others and gaining confidence and security in these relationships.

Action plan: We created the following action plan together.

1. *Examine motivations and intentions.* What did he want? How did he know when he got it? Why did he do the things he did? What was important to him? What were his priorities?

2. *Change the thoughts.* He had to learn to deal with his emotions. Instead of thinking, "They don't need me anymore," he learned to think, "I am still part of this family" or "I have a loving family."

3. *Change the behavior.* He began to do things like taking his family out to dinner, going on vacations with them, and having date nights with his wife. He learned to do things that affirmed his new commitment to his family. Using those techniques, he gradually strengthened his relationships with those close to him.

Self-Reflection: Looking Inward and Outward

Even though we are heavily influenced by the people closest to us, we are the only ones who can live our lives. Sometimes we need to tend to our own business. You can do this easily by having your own personal counseling sessions with a very wise soul—your own.

Exercise: Wise Counsel

For any problem that you have, or for any thought that you want to change or analyze, you can start a counseling session inside your head with this wiser part of yourself. Let me demonstrate. (In the following dialogue, and in similar dialogues throughout the book, I identify the wise voice of your soul as the "counselor self" and your everyday consciousness as just "myself"—abbreviated as CS and MS, respectively.)

MS—I can't believe she did that! She is so hateful!

CS—*Is being angry with her helpful to you in any way?*

MS—I don't care if it is helpful. I am justified.

CS—*I am not arguing that point. I simply asked a question. Let me rephrase it for you. Is it good for your health to stay angry about this for days and days? Will it change what happened?*

MS—No, but I will feel better knowing that she deserves such bad thoughts.

CS—*Yes, but they don't hurt her nearly as much as they hurt you. You are the one sending out negativity now—not her. You will be the one who gets back what you give out. She may feel your anger, but you will feel it stronger and longer. It is much more adaptive for you to let go of this anger and cease to allow it to harm either of you. Two wrongs do not make a right. Remember?*

MS—I guess you are right. It is just so hard to let go. She really is mean!

CS—*You cannot change who she is anymore than she can change you. You also cannot be responsible for her behavior. You can only own your own. Do not let her get to you like that. She is not worth it.*

MS—You can say that again. She is not worth any of my attention.

CS—*You have the answer then. Do not give her any of your attention.*

MS—Thank you. That is good advice—even if it easier said than done.

CS—*It is only as hard as you make it. It is all in your mind, you know.*

You can apply this sort of session to any number of problems that you might face. The point is to boil the issue down to its essence. What is the bottom line? Then think it through in a logical manner, considering everything involved. Here is another example.

MS—"What should I do?"

CS—*What do you feel in your heart?*

MS—Hmm ... I feel like I should let go and move on. That is what my heart says, but my mind says it is not ready to stop thinking about it just yet. My mind is somewhat fixated on this, and wants its turn creating false realities and making things up.

CS—*If you let go, you would have to think about something else. Move on. You recognize that you might have a hard time doing this.*

MS—Exactly.

CS—*So, find something new to think about first. Focus on something different. Find a new cause to spark your interest.*

MS—What?

CS—*Find a new thought. For instance, ask yourself "What do I really want?" and answer that question. Explore various options and play out various scenarios. Just get your mind on something else.*

MS—OK, so I take my mind off of it now, but that doesn't make it go away. It is still there.

CS—*You are right, it is still there. But when you put it in the background, it loses influence in your life. Accept only positive influences in your life. Rid yourself of the negative. Think forward and upward. Think love and light.*

MS—OK, so I move it to the background and continue living on—creating something new and better along the way. Thank you. I will try.

CS—*Change that to present tense positive, and I will accept it. How about, "I am trying," or better yet, "I am allowing things to get better in my life."*

MS—Wow. That's hard, but it does feel good. I am trying. I am allowing things to get better. I allow good to come into my life, and I know I deserve it. I take responsibility for my life and my behavior. I choose to make it better.

CS—*Good. Now go into your life and create something new.*

Soul Lessons

There are certain paths in your life that you are led to by your soul. Taking them always leads to light.

Inspire to make a difference. When you can, anytime you see an opportunity, inspire someone to be more. Inspire yourself to do more. Realize that you can make a difference, and recognize that if you don't, who will?

Aspire to beauty. Aim to bring beauty into your awareness whenever possible. See the colors in things, and appreciate the hues. Recognize the dimensions, and appreciate the layers of life all around you.

Recognize your capacity to love. You have an incredible capacity to love. You can never run out of love. It continually renews itself and increases exponentially as you go. Give love whenever you can. There will always be more where that came from.

Shine your light always. Bring light into your life and spread it all around. It not only feels good, it is good.

Be part of the solution, not part of the problem. Focus on solution-based thinking. What can you do to make a situation any better than it is now? Become part of the solution whenever you can. You don't have to contribute to the problem.

Express yourself creatively. It is good to express yourself and your uniqueness. Find a creative outlet for this self-expression. Whether it be art or exercise, politics or pottery, find a way to tell the world what you have to say.

Practice loving kindness. You have opportunities to express love and/or kindness throughout each day. When it is easy and feels right, express this loving kindness to anyone around you. Your kindness will come back to you tenfold.

Value your individualism and uniqueness. Value who you are. You are the only one just like you. You are special and unique and very loved. Be proud of yourself and all that you have created in your life. If you are not proud of it, it is never too late to change it.

Shared Reality

5

Defining Shared Reality

What is reality? What is *real*?

Having spent much of my adult life in pursuit of the answer to this question, I have consolidated a theory about shared reality. This theory contains five basic tenets that describe the operation of the world around us. They are:

1. We have free will.
2. What goes around comes around.
3. Life exists on a continuum.
4. Energy never dies; it simply changes form.
5. There is a higher power that transcends all and yet exists in all.

Part Two of this book not only explains my theory of external/shared reality, it also teaches you how to use these ideas to create a better personal reality for yourself. I draw on the principles of cognitive-behavioral therapy to teach you to recognize your current thought patterns and learn to change them. You'll also learn fun, easy, and creative exercises that take little time and produce immediate results. You'll instantly feel better, and you can use these techniques anywhere, at any time.

The exercises will assist you in changing your reality by opening the door to new thought processes. You will begin to recognize your mind's role in the reality that you experience, and you will learn how to control your thoughts. You can change your reality, and you can change your life.

Only you can control what goes on inside your head. Since you can control your thoughts, why not make them more positive, life-affirming, and abundant? Why not control your thoughts and use them to your advantage?

While the first part of this book was about your personal reality, this part focuses on the reality that we all share with those around us. You will see how important it becomes to surround yourself with positive influences, and you will recognize the value of your surroundings. You will begin to better appreciate those loving aspects in your life, and begin to recognize just how fortunate you are to have certain people in your life. And you will remember to cherish the times that you have together.

Let's get to it! It is time to create the reality that you desire.

6

Free Will

We have the will and the freedom to do whatever we want to do, whenever we want to do it. This does not imply that we will not suffer consequences for our actions (for we inevitably will), but we do have the freedom to make those choices and to take those actions. We have the freedom to choose our thoughts, to control our emotions, and to modify our reactions.

It takes practice to learn to do this effectively, but it can be done. You *can* control what goes on inside your mind. You may have allowed someone else to do this for you thus far, but you can begin today—at this moment—to do it on your own.

Sure, people can—and do—tell us how to think, but they cannot *make* us think in those ways. No one stops us from doing what we truly want to do. Laws, rules, and discipline may guide us to make certain decisions, and define consequences for certain dangerous actions, but the ultimate decisions are ours. This is free will in action.

"But," you may be arguing, "if I truly had free will, then I could do whatever I wanted, and that's crazy. How can I control my boss?"

I did not say that you could control "people" or "things." I said that you could control *yourself*—your thoughts, your emotions, your reactions, your behavior. You may have little actual control over your environment, your circumstances, or certain situations you find yourself in, but you do have *total* control over your reactions to these things, and your behaviors that stem from them.

Let me give you an example. Say that you perceive your boss or someone in your life to be mean and hateful. You find yourself thinking often of how much you dislike this person, and wishing that he would go away. You obsess over this. Thinking about him makes you cringe or seethe with anger. Now, let's add that he has a pretty solid place in your life—there is no easy escape from him. You must be around him a lot.

How do you exercise free will in this case, you ask. The answer: you have free will in every way that it exists.

1. You can always *change the circumstance* itself through which you are attached to this person (in this case, leave the job). This is often traumatic, however, and not easily accomplished (you need that money or those benefits, for example). You may also end up attracting a similar person in your new circumstances, for we continue repeating lessons in our life until we learn them.

2. You can *change some behavior* or way of interacting with the person, and thus minimize the conflict between you. If your boss drives you crazy wanting to know what you have accomplished, beat him to the punch by sending him a regular update on your workload. Doing *something—anything—* different is often all that is needed to break a bad pattern of relating.

3. You can *change your thoughts*. Sometimes what is wrong with a situation is your thinking about the situation. If you see something as a challenge, rather than a problem, it takes on a whole new meaning. If you see something as a lesson

rather than a punishment, it feels different. If you think that someone is being hard on you to help you in the long run, it feels different than if you perceive that this person is being hard on you to get rid of you. Remember that what doesn't kill us makes us stronger. You can use this affirmation as a mantra for self-empowerment. Your interactions with this person are probably not going to kill you. Yet, if you learn from these interactions, you will likely become stronger. Examine what you are thinking in any situation to know if it is emotionally healthy for you or not. Even when you cannot change a situation, *you can change how you think about it.*

4. You can *change your feelings*, or reactions, or emotions. This is a little harder for some people, but it *is* possible. Most likely, you will have to change how you think about something first; then it becomes easier to feel differently. Thoughts and feelings go hand in hand, for your feelings are the results of your thoughts. The fastest way to change the way you feel is to pick a different way to feel, and concentrate on this new feeling intently for several minutes. For example, if you are mad, you can *decide* (a thought) to let go of this anger by thinking about something funny (or another "opposite" emotion) and concentrating on that image intently. Soon, you will have a smile on your face. You could also pick a loving image to focus on (such as holding your child as a baby, or smelling a flower) and begin to feel warmth and surrender and joy. Whatever feeling you pick, you have the ability to change emotional states *at will.* You may argue that this feeling of joy is not real, and that you are making this feeling up in your mind. Well, you made up the angry feelings also; you just did that subconsciously, based on a learned pattern of responding. Changing the emotion is something you are doing consciously and *at will.* You are

practicing your ability to create a new reality in this moment. You are taking charge of your mind, instead of allowing old patterns to create your present reality for you.

The point is that you can change several different things or you can change nothing at all. Either way, it is your choice. You are not at the mercy of every circumstance in your life. You have control over what you think and how you feel. You have control over yourself. Let me show you how you can begin to use this control.

Why Free Will?

Free will is an excellent teaching tool. By making our own mistakes, we learn. Through learning, we grow. In growing, we fill with more light and love. As we fill with light and love, we spread more light and love. We become better able to share our love and our emotions with others. You can help change the world by changing yourself.

Don't Let Fear Stop You

If you find yourself worrying or hating, stop yourself, and do something different. Ask for light, keep an open mind, and keep your thoughts positive. If the questions or thoughts continue to plague you, answer them. Ask yourself what you are really afraid of. Explore what comes into your mind. Why is this so scary to you?

As you dig deeper into your fears, you may find an undercurrent of fears about love. The fear of love has many faces: fear of rejection, fear of never truly knowing love, fear of abandonment, and fear of not being able to love. Fear—not hate—is the opposite of love. Hate incorporates passion, and that is a form of love. There is no love in fear. You end fear by facing it. It loses all of its power that way. Recognize your fears for what they are, and stand up to them. Send light to your fears. Intend to transcend them. Have faith that everything is going be OK—however it turns out. Know that the universe loves and supports you no matter what happens. Know that you are never alone.

Free Will Extends into the Family

"If I have free will," you might ask, "why was I born into the family I have?" You were born into a family and a set of circumstances. You are here to live with them and share with them and learn with them. You have lots of issues to work though. A history exists among you that you may not even be consciously aware of, yet you know there is a reason they are in your life.

Why do you feel so strongly towards these people? Why can't you break away from them? You are connected to them—spiritually—at a soul level. You are here to help each other out, to teach each other lessons, and to experience life together. You are here to love and support one another. Even when the circumstances are bad between you, you still feel this connection at the soul level. These people remain in your heart and are often in your mind. You care for these people deeply, even when they frustrate and anger you. You travel together through time, sometimes closer, and sometimes drifting apart. Yet, in your heart, you know that these people are always with you. A part of them lives inside you.

Within this context of family and loved ones, you use your free will. The circumstances have been set for you. This is the place in which you live, and these are the people you share life with. Yet, how you behave within this environment, what you choose to do with your life, is still your decision. Lots of factors influence you, but you ultimately act of your own volition.

Until you recognize that you have free will, you may fail to use it; or—just as bad—you may continue to be controlled by outside influences. If your outside influences are not good, then your choices will likely be bad ones. Being blind to this tenet is harmful to your mental health.

It may be easier to be told what to do and how to think, but it is not mentally healthy. We, as a society, allow ourselves to be manipulated; we allow the media and the people around us to tell us what to think and how to feel. We accept the information these sources give us without question, and allow the presenter's view to become our own. We get so busy that even thinking through a problem seems like an insurmountable task. Our minds are too cluttered to sort it all out, so we just accept what is given without question.

Knowing the beauty of free will and choice changes all of this. New possibilities appear in all directions when we open our eyes to see them. We begin to recognize what we can change and what we cannot. We learn when to surrender and when to fight like hell. We learn to invoke the serenity prayer: to accept those things that cannot be changed, change the things that we can change, and find the wisdom to know the difference.

7

What Goes Around Comes Around

What *goes around comes around. Do unto others as you would have done unto you. You reap what you sow. For every action, there is an equal and opposite reaction. Karma. You get back what you give out.*

No matter how—or how many times—it is said, the idea is the same, and it is perhaps the most golden rule of all. God, or some powerful external force, does not punish you for your wrongdoings; you do it to yourself. You create a continuum of energy that guides you into your future with your thoughts, actions, and intentions. You create and continuously recreate your reality with these tools.

The energy you send out—the essence or feeling or intent behind the actions—is what you attract back to yourself. Your actions and words and thoughts are mirrored back to you in your surroundings. You notice them more clearly because you resonate with them. You recognize them. You feel them at an energy level, for they match your energy.

If you make a conscious effort to think positive thoughts or imagine brighter images, then brighter images will be mirrored back to you. You will see a little bit of good in things today, and even a little bit more tomorrow. The more you look for the good, the more you will find.

Unfortunately the same is true for negative thinking. Once you begin to dwell on a negative thought, you allow it to consume you and become part of your reality. Once it takes hold, the pattern simply repeats itself, keeping you stuck in the darkness.

It is *in your mind* that these patterns are occurring. It is *only* in your mind that you can change them. You are the only person *in the whole world* who can control your thoughts. No one else can control them for you! Only you dictate what is said inside your head. Thoughts may run rampant in there, but you have the ability to tame them. And you allow them in; otherwise, they would not be there.

As soon as you decide to move forward, you can begin to change your thoughts to better serve you. Then there will be growth. Growth is expansion and a willingness to keep an open mind. You may not know—may never know—all of the answers, yet there is a certainty that everything will be OK. You learn to develop trust, and you gain a sense of security in your ability to affect your reality in a positive way. You become more aware and have clarity about each of your options. You see things more clearly. You learn from the mistakes of others without having to make them yourself.

The Evolution of a Thought

Here are a few examples of how your thoughts become your reality. Notice the difference in reality when your attitude changes.

Example 1: Evolution of a Thought

If you continuously think about how bad everything around you is, you stay steeped in a murky emotional turmoil that says, "This is bad and it's getting worse." Your reality will reflect your belief.

Yet, by changing your "reality mantra," you change your whole experience. What if you modified the thought just slightly by thinking, "This is bad, but I can find a way to make it better"? Or, "This may be bad now, but it is getting better"?

You change the thought gradually with minor changes that are believable to you. The eventual goal is to have a thought that is present tense and of a positive focus. At first you may not even have to believe this new thought for it to help you, but you do need to allow the thought to evolve to a higher form.

An eventual acceptable thought might be: "While I may not like the circumstances I find myself in, I am willing to take what responsibility I have to change things for the better. I recognize that these things must be happening for a reason, and I seek now to learn what I can, so not to have to repeat this."

An even higher thought might be: "I am continuously evolving and growing. I see every experience in my life as a learning opportunity. I appreciate this opportunity to move forward and upward."

Example 2: Evolution of a Thought

Original thought: "There is not enough. How will we ever make it? What are we going to do?" (Remember: The circumstances don't have to change for your thoughts about them to change. One is not dependent on the other.)

First modification: Attempt to make the statement a little more positive, while still being reasonable and still believing yourself. "I need to take a good look at things and be open to creative solutions that are good for everyone involved." Begin to allow yourself to believe that there is hope in the situation.

Further modification: Allow the possibility that things can get better. "It may not feel like it now, but I know that on some level there is enough. We have food to eat. We have shelter over our heads. There is hope. I will find some way to solve this problem."

Even further modification: "There is enough. There is always enough. I may not have everything I want, but at least I always know that there is enough to get by. At a fundamental level, I am provided for. I have enough." (Present tense; more reality based; more positive focus.)

Positive thought/focus: "I am abundantly provided for. I have everything I need."

The concept consists of examining your thought processes to determine which thoughts are unhealthy or harmful to you or your emotional health. Once you recognize that a thought pattern is taking you nowhere positive, you can begin to change those thoughts to ones that will serve you better.

It is really a matter of master and servant. Are you the master of your mind—or a servant to your mind's ranting and ravings? Only you can answer this question for yourself. Only you can change your role from one to the other.

"What Goes Around Comes Around" in Action

Perhaps the most immediate example of this tenet is the smile. If you smile at people, they generally smile back. Even if they do not know you or think you are strange for smiling at them, they will usually smile back. You are spreading light with that smile. People can't help but respond to that. They catch the light you send, and that light is reciprocated.

The same is true for anger or sad emotions. If someone is displaying a strong emotion in your presence, you can't help but feel that emotion. You respond to it at a physical and emotional level, either by feeling the same emotion or by noticing that you are uncomfortable feeling the other person's emotion. If you are around someone who is angry, your body may tense in a physical reaction, while emotionally, you become guarded and defensive. If you have a strong will or are trained to help people, then you may be able to detach from that emotion to be more available for that person. If you don't know how to detach, though, you seem to catch that emotion like you would catch a cold.

This explains why you are sometimes uncomfortable around a person, even when you don't know why. That person may be experiencing something at an emotional level that she is giving off, and you, as a sensitive and caring person, are picking up on that emotion.

There is energy in emotion, just as there is energy in all life. Energy has greatly varying frequencies, and moves at different speeds depending on the emotion being expressed. You resonate with some of these frequencies more easily than others. The higher and finer frequencies are available to you through focused intent. All you have to do is think of an emotion or an emotional state like peace, love, or joy. Concentrate on that emotion, and you begin to feel and experience the essence of that emotion. Concentrate on it more intently or more frequently, and you make it bigger. You can experience any emotion, whenever you want, wherever you want.

Abundance Thinking

The reciprocal nature of energy seems to be especially true with money. When someone gives money (or food or shelter) to someone else in need—even if they don't really have it to give— it seems to find its way back to them in some form. Money flows in and out of our lives. It is not a constant. Its energy moves— sometimes we are bringing it in, and other times we are sending it out. Like attracts like. When we are open and giving, that flow of money in our lives is more open and giving. If we are stingy and greedy, our energy is more closed off. It is harder for new money to find us when we are hoarding and protecting all that we have.

Of course it is wise to save money, invest wisely, and have some reserved for a rainy day. Wisdom and greed are two separate things. But if you have something that someone else needs more than you do at the moment, then what harm does it do to share? That person may not repay you, but the universe will for your kind and open heart. The next time you need something, you will receive it—sometimes in the most unexpected ways.

You don't have to become a saint for this to happen. You don't have to quit your job, or devote every free moment to charity efforts and volunteer work. Do what you can, but also know your limits. If you are not taking care of yourself, then how can you take care of so many others? You must put your health—your mental, emotional, and physical health—on the front burner. Take care of yourself first—by allowing light and love into your heart and life.

You Create Your Future by the Choices You Make Today

You are currently and continuously creating your reality with your thoughts, perceptions, actions, words, and emotions. Each moment that you experience is, at least in part, your own creation.

Here are some simple techniques to change your personal reality.

1. *Monitor your thoughts and make changes as necessary.* The next time you find yourself experiencing a moment that you don't really like, ask yourself what is going on, and what about it you don't like. Spend a few minutes in self-analysis, and take stock of what is going on in your head. Does it

WHAT GOES AROUND COMES AROUND

help the situation in any way? Are you contributing to the resolution of the issue in any way? What doesn't feel right about this?

When you find answers you are looking for, modify your thinking to match this new concept. You can't change a negative pattern without identifying it first. Yet, you cannot stop with identification—you must acknowledge and then move on. If necessary, modify it every step of the way.

2. *Think forward and upward.* When in doubt about what to do, think forward and upward. Move courageously onward into the future with hope and strength and knowing. What can be wrong with that?

3. *When there is a choice between light and darkness, choose light.* It doesn't get much simpler than that.

4. *Find faith or hope in something positive and life affirming, and maintain it.* Research shows that it doesn't matter so much *what* you have faith in, as long as you have it. Find security in something that is meaningful and full of promise. It's good for your health—both physical and emotional.

What About Tragedy?

I'm not saying that you purposely "bring on" the bad things in your life. I do not feel that you ever *deserve* to have anything bad happen to you. Just because something tragic has happened in your life, it does not necessarily mean that you are being punished for some past mistake. Maybe you are, but maybe you just needed something like this to happen to aim you in a new direction, or to move you to a new place in life. This thing has happened for some reason. You may not know what that is—now or ever—but there is a reason. Everything has its purpose, and there is ultimate harmony in all things.

Again, we do not control all of the circumstances in our lives. Some things are beyond our reach. Some things can't be immediately explained. Some things are part of a bigger plan that we can't completely comprehend. Sometimes, things just stink.

What we *can* get out of tragedy, though, is growth—and movement forward. We can get to a place in which we can accept that our faith is enough to get us through. We can decide that we don't have to *know* right now *why* this happened. All we have to do is accept that it did happen, learn what we can from it, and decide if there is anything we can do to prevent it from happening again.

Did this tragedy bring you closer to anyone? Did it draw someone new into your life, who might be there to help you grow in some way? Or help you with a lesson of some kind? Did you find your faith again, or see some miracle happen in spite of the pain? Perhaps this thing pushed you in a new direction—led you toward a new path.

Significant events define our lives. We remember the big things in our past much more clearly than the small ones. Each of those big events opened new or different doors for us. Things happened that might not have happened otherwise.

You can almost think of each event as a signal that steers you toward another direction. This thing happens, and suddenly you are living in a different world. You feel like you've entered another life. Your future is suddenly less predictable. You begin to wonder what will happen next.

In this space in time, your life has changed. And many, many doors have just opened. The choices you make, and the actions you take, lead you through one of those doors. And you are set in a whole new direction. Maybe that is good, or maybe you perceive it as very bad, but either way a shift is occurring.

Recognize your control while this is happening. If the time has already passed, look at it from hindsight and notice how things changed after this event. If you wish they had changed in a different way, explore that train of thought and examine if that really would have been any better in the end. Then realize that it is never too late to move on. What has happened in the past is over with. It can only control your present to the extent that you allow it to. Choose a new path if you desire. Decide that you are going to see the value of this thing in some way, and attempt to allow it less room in your current awareness.

Perhaps you have learned a virtue from this event. Patience, hope, unconditional love—these are all best learned first-hand. It is difficult to have a concept of hope if you have never felt it. Embracing a positive value gives new meaning to life. You feel something new. And this feeling is lighter and brighter and nicer. You consciously choose it and feel good about that.

Get what you can from your past. Look for its lessons. Then move on. Allow it to be something that is part of your past, *not your present*. Put it in a box on the closet shelf, out of sight; it will still be there if you ever need to go back to it. You don't have to carry it around with you forever. You are able to put it in its place; let it serve its purpose and then move on. And if one day you are ready to clean out the closet and throw the box away, you will be able to do so with no problems. You just know you don't need it taking up space anymore and you bid it good-bye. You let go and move on.

Life occurs in the present moment. What is past is past; the future is yet to come. Now is all we really have. How are things *now* in your life? How do you feel at this very moment? Is that how you want to feel? I hope that you are beginning to see some options. I hope that you are getting rid of the ghosts that haunt you, and living more *in this reality, at this time*.

Techniques for Healing

1. *Be honest with yourself,* but don't judge yourself too harshly. You are human and therefore allowed to make mistakes.

2. *Take responsibility for your behaviors.* No matter what you have done, accept that you did it and that you can't go back and change it. You can, however, mold and shape your future. Begin to take responsibility for your life *now*, and your future can only get brighter.

3. *Forgive yourself.* It won't matter if others forgive you if you can't forgive yourself. Know that you were doing the best you knew how to at the time. Recognize that you are your harshest judge, and dismiss all charges on yourself.

4. *Get rid of the negativity in your life*, but be careful not to spread it. Send all negativity of any kind far away from you. Send it to the Universal Recycling Center for transformation into reusable energy.

5. *Do something nice for yourself.* You've survived. You deserve it.

6. *Give thanks for all you do have.* No matter how bad it gets, it could be worse. Be thankful for everything that is working in your life.

7. *Appreciate what you have instead of focusing on what you lack.* Remember—what you think about, you create. If you continuously remind yourself how lucky you are, you will automatically *feel* more lucky.

8. *Give and share with others.* Giving is healing.

9. *Allow good into your life.* Remind yourself that you are just as worthy as anyone else. There is enough to go around, but you must allow it to come into your life.

10. *Love yourself.* You are special and unique. If you can't love yourself, how can others love you?

8

Life Exists on a Continuum

We've learned thus far that free will makes us responsible for our actions, and the cycle of life helps us to learn and grow. Within this framework of life, though, we feel a need to define things and categorize them as desirable or undesirable. Dualities exist to help us define things.

All things exist on a continuum from one extreme to the other. To define what any point on the continuum is like, you have to compare it to the other points on the continuum. To know what "thin" looks like, you have to have some idea of what "fat" looks like. And it is just that—an idea. "Thin" does not have an absolute standard that defines it; what is "thin" for one person may be "fat" for another. Society may adopt basic standards that suggest something is thin or fat, but there is no definition without comparison.

Much of life is subjective in this way. Much of how you perceive depends on your thoughts, and on the comparisons that you make in your mind. If you change your thoughts, your whole perception of something changes. You see it in a new way.

Imagine life on this continuum: a long line that extends left to right, with darkness on the far left and bright light on the far right. At the dark end lies fear, hate, greed, selfish desire, loathing, guilt, and sorrow—heavy emotions that weigh us down and try to drown us. Toward the middle, balance, peace, and harmony appear. There is an acceptance that there are things both good and bad, but there is a balance between them. Toward the far right is love, light, hope, and sunshine. These are light and airy emotions of a finer and higher vibration. When you feel them, your whole body feels lighter and your spirit feels more free.

All life exists on this continuum, with some of us living closer to one end than the other. If you hate your brother, then you are hating some part of yourself—for you both lie on this same continuum. Even if he lives far away from you, you are both on this line together.

When you dislike someone or something, there is something about that energy that makes you uncomfortable. Some psychological buttons are being pushed. You dislike this feeling and take it as a reason to be afraid. Fear leads to apprehension and distrust. Fear always lies beneath hate.

Certain tenets of physics seem to apply to our thoughts as well as the energy around us. For example, "What you resist, persists," and "What you push away, gets pushed back at you." Do either of these ideas push your emotional buttons? My advice is to stop resisting what you do not want. Release its hold on you by accepting it as a part of life, and know that it can only affect you to the extent that you allow it to. When you can send light and good thoughts to your enemies, you have risen to a new level. Think good thoughts for everyone involved in any situation.

Positive Affirmations

Repeating positive thoughts in your mind helps you to retrain your brain toward brighter thinking. You can repeat the following affirmations to yourself anytime and anywhere. Please feel free to modify them to better suit your personal style of thinking or your personal belief system. These are simply examples to get you started.

- I surround and protect myself with light and love.
- I allow light to shine within and through me.
- I invite and allow more light and love into my life.
- I recognize my abundance and am thankful for all that I have.
- I appreciate my life and the people who share it with me.
- I recognize my choices in all situations.
- I recognize my level of control in all situations.

Where We Are

At this moment, there is a lot that we don't yet know. I find it helpful to accept that there is a flow of light that runs through all life—an energy. From this we can each create our own theory about the way things are.

We can each look at our lives and decide how we want to feel and how we want to act. We can begin to examine our thoughts, recognize what is really going on in all that background noise, and finally change it. We don't have to change anything major, we just have to change a single thought. Let's think a single new thought, and see where it takes us. If we don't like where it takes us, we simply choose another path and think a new thought. We begin to see things in a new light.

If something bad happens, we try to recuperate from it and move forward, knowing we have love and support every step of the way. There is obviously some reason for this thing, so we might as well just go with the flow. We don't have to know all of the answers. Sometimes, praying for light to enter the situation is the best that we can do.

Putting Things into Perspective

This example illustrates what you can do if you find that you don't like something or someone, and have just accepted that without exploring the reasons for your dislike. In this case, I kept noticing that every time I was around a certain person, I became very uncomfortable and agitated. Being the good counselor that I am, I asked myself . . .

CS—*What is it about this person that gives you the heebie-jeebies every time you are around him? Tell me about this.*

MS—Well, for starters, he is crude, rude, cocky, and a real smart aleck.

CS—*So, what you dislike or find offensive is his behavior—crudeness, rudeness, cockiness, and smart-aleckiness?*

MS—You're right. I don't like his behavior, but I also just don't like him.

CS—*What is it about him that you don't like?*

MS—I don't like his attitude. I don't agree with his view of life.

CS—*As, I am sure, he doesn't agree with yours.*

MS—Exactly.

CS—*But there are many people whose views of life are different from yours. You are two different people. Of course you are not going to agree on everything. What is so different about this person?*

MS—I don't have a problem with him being his own person. I have a problem with him being in my life. He is here to stay whether I like it or not, so how am I going to learn to live with that?

CS—*Stop taking this so personally. The way he is, is the way he is—whether you are in his life or not. You are not responsible for his behavior, and you do not have to tolerate it in your life. But, you are* right, he is in your life. So, it might be a good idea to learn to at least be civil in his presence.

You need to pay attention to and become aware of your reactions and behaviors in his presence. Ask yourself why something bothers you, and see if you can't figure out what it is that is so upsetting. You need to examine why you let these things bother you.

MS—It bothers me because he is offensive and hurts people with his words. This is not right, and he shouldn't do it.

CS—So is your dislike of his behavior going to make him change it?

MS—I doubt it.

CS—OK. So you want your judgment of him to hurt him like he hurts others?

MS—Well, no. I just would like him to see what he is doing to himself and the people around him. I would like him to recognize the effects of his actions.

CS—Do you think he will? Do you think that you are conveying this information to him in such a way that he understands what you are saying?

MS—I doubt it.

CS—Do you think that you can change him?

MS—No. I know I can't change him. He has to change himself. He has to own what is his, just like I can only own what is mine. I might be able to help him recognize what he is doing though. Maybe then he would see, and change of his own accord.

CS—Are you doing this?

MS—No. I am avoiding him because I don't like his energy. And when I am around him, I am just irritated.

CS—At least you recognize that. And you are right, you can't do it for him. When you are ready, though, you might be able to help him in some way. You both are in each other's lives for some reason. Your paths have *crossed at this time and in this place by some grander design. Maybe he is here to teach you a new tolerance, or a new way of relating to others. Maybe he is showing you what your buttons are, and how easily they are pushed. There are always lessons that you can bring out of any negative situation. You just have to be aware and open to seeing these messages.*

Let's do a quick exercise to illustrate something you can do about this situation right now.

Remember the continuum we talked about earlier? Imagine this continuum now. It goes from darkness on the left to bright light on the right.

Each of you is a person, and all people exist on the same continuum of light. Imagine where your place is on this continuum and see yourself standing there for a moment. Now, place this other person on the continuum where you might imagine him to be. This is where this person stands in your life. Notice where he is. Is he close to you? Or far away? Is he in a darker area than you? Or brighter?

Now, send love to this person down the continuum.

MS—But . . .

CS—*No buts. Pay attention. Send love (or light, if love is too difficult to muster) down the continuum. Let him know—at an energy level—that you have no problems with him. You mean no harm to him and wish that he mean no harm to you. Clear the air between you. Let him know that you are just trying to survive like he is, and that you want what is best for everyone involved. Let go of any residual anger or similar energy you feel toward this person.*

A good way to let this energy go is to imagine all of the negativity you feel for this person going down your arm into a laser gun you are holding in your hand. All of the energy builds up in this gun. You then aim the gun up into the sky, and begin to shoot the energy out toward the sky. Mentally tell this energy to go to the Universal Recycling Center for transformation into light. Shoot the energy away with a one-way ticket to eternity. Zap all of the negative energy, all of the hate and disgust and distrust, into the sky. Zap the loathing. Let it all go.

Tell the person that you are releasing any hold he may have on you. If you've felt held by this relationship in any way, release that now. Tear it off. If there are ropes, cut or untie them. If there is heaviness or darkness, wash it off.

Put it in a hot air balloon or simply zap it into the stars. Send it to the Universal Recycling Center in your mind. It will go there. Let the light take care of it from here. Get rid of it, let it go, and then allow yourself to heal. Release the hold this person has on you, and feel how good it feels to be released.

MS—You're right. That does feel better.

Visualizations of Light

You can bring light into your life in many different ways. Following are some short visualizations that can be used anytime and anywhere to bring light and love into your physical presence. While these comprise many visual and kinesthetic options, you may create another image of your very own. Whatever the image, allow the purpose to remain the same—to increase a feeling of light or brightness in your life.

Dimmer Switch Visualization

Imagine a dimmer switch—the circular light switch that allows you to adjust the brightness of the light in a room. Imagine this switch representing a continuum of light. When it is turned all the way to the left, the light is off. When you turn it to the right, first it clicks on, and then it adjusts the brightness as you turn it clockwise. The continuum exists between being off, and being as bright as it can be.

Imagine that the light in your life or in the room around you can be controlled with this switch. Turn this light on, and adjust it to the brightness you currently feel. Find a level that is comfortable and feels right for this time and space. Notice how this level compares to your everyday level. Decide that you are going to turn up this light, just a bit. Adjust its light, brighter, until it feels like that is enough. Notice how it feels to be brighter.

You can adjust this level of light in your life anytime. You can always turn it up or down to suit your liking. You control how much of what you have in your life on an energy level—in your mind. After something is established on an energy level, then it can come through to the physical.

Sliding Switch Visualization

For this visualization, imagine a sliding light switch, with markings that describe in increments the amount of light being given out at any time. This continuum is marked on a scale of 1–100, where 1 is total darkness and 100 is total brightness. When you turn on the switch, find the number you are at now. Is it 24? 46? 63? 82? What feels descriptive of your place now? After you've found your current number, decide to turn it up to some higher number. What feels right to you? 10 notches higher? 20? Notice how your body and the space around you feel different at one number than at another. Do you feel better when you are close to the middle of the scale? Or brighter?

Make it a goal to stay at or above 50 as much as possible. When you notice that you are falling well below that, consciously turn it up. 50 is just half; halfway between light and darkness. Strive to move toward the light; feel how good it feels to turn it up.

Do this exercise several times a day. It only takes a few seconds to notice where you are at on the scale and decide to turn it up. Even noticing where you are at is beneficial to your mental health. You are checking in with yourself and seeing how you are doing. Awareness is necessary for any change to occur. You have to know where you are, to know where you are trying to get.

Sunshine Visualization

Imagine that you are standing outside on a beautiful spring day. The sun is shining brightly overhead, and you are thankful for its warmth. You stand with your face to the sun. Closing your eyes, you allow the sunshine to wash over you and fill you with its warmth and energy. You appreciate the sun for its role in providing light and opportunities for growth. You recognize the incredible significance of the sun for our survival. You bask in its glow.

Turning on the Headlights

Imagine turning on the headlights of your car—even if it is in the middle of the day. Thank your headlights for illuminating what it is front of you and for assisting in guiding your way. Know that your path is well lit, and trust that you can see what is coming your way.

9

Energy Never Dies;
It Simply Changes Form

Energy never dies; it simply changes form. This is a theory of physics that also applies to spirituality. In physics, an atom never ceases to be an atom. It never dies or disappears. The Law of Conservation of Energy tells us that it may change forms, but it always exists. We are made up of atoms. Our bodies, our organs, our essence are all made up of these tiny particles of life. This energy of life may leave our bodies when we die, but it does not just evaporate into thin air. It lives on as energy.

Your thoughts and actions and emotions also have energy; this energy also moves and lives on. In fact, your energy is often contagious. Have you ever been around someone who is excited, and you got excited too? Have you ever been around someone who was worried or scared, and you felt physical reactions—like a stomach ache, or tension in your head? Have you ever walked into a room and felt like there had just been an argument there? Or felt a sense of peace, or longing?

It is important to recognize your power and energy so that you can begin to control it. If you don't believe this, consider one of your close relationships. Imagine this person to whom you are close, and imagine a time when you could read them so well that you knew what they were thinking without them having to express it out loud. You could almost hear their thoughts, and you reached out to them with your comfort or empathy. This is possible because emotions and thoughts have an energy of their own. Parents pick up on this, for example, as they watch their children lie to them. Something is "said" that goes beyond the words or the body language itself. An energy is expressed that is more than the form of expression itself.

It is important to learn to work on your own thoughts and control your own emotions. When you begin to see your patterns of thinking and your problem areas, you can then begin to change them. And when you are helping yourself, you are helping everyone around you. Your energy is contagious. When your energy is good, you send goodness out into the space around you.

When you clear your energy space, others feel the difference and want to clear theirs also. As they said in the '70s, you begin to give off "good vibes." Light creates more light.

This brings us to the concept of the ripple effect.

The Ripple Effect

When a pebble is dropped into still water, many tiny waves ripple out from the center where it was dropped. The ripple of that pebble being dropped reaches out far beyond the place where it landed in the water. This one action has far-reaching effects.

Likewise, when we say or do something, the effects of those words or actions reach far beyond their intended target.

When you smile at a stranger in the grocery store and that person smiles back, you can see the glow she felt in response to your kind gesture, and you sense her gratitude. She then carries that glow with her to spread it to other people, and they in turn spread it to others.

By the same token, when you bite someone's head off with a sharp comment, you see that person shrink back and begin guarding herself for more attacks. She then carries that tension with her into the rest of her day. The ripple effects from that one exchange may be carried around for months or years to come, depending on the emotional health of that person.

I am sure you can think of something that you did or said many, many years ago that still affects you today. We still remember and regret silly things from our past; we hold onto them, and remind ourselves of our stupidity whenever we get the chance. Events of the past still live in the present because we allow them to come back into our lives. And when they come back, they bring all of their emotional baggage with them. You think of an event and feel the years of pain and regret and guilt and stupidity all over again.

This is further proof that thoughts and emotions carry energy. They live on. They exist all around us. We continuously feed them and allow them to survive.

For you to gain control over your mental health and emotional well-being, you have to accept this as true and learn to work with it. When you learn to change your thoughts—or at least learn to recognize and question them—you begin to improve your mental health. As you improve yourself and your thoughts, you automatically help those around you.

Client Example. I had a client who was working through the shock having been left by his wife of twenty-four years. He had never imagined life without her, and had taken for granted that she'd always be there. Now he had lots of time to look back on how things had gone so wrong.

When questioned about his goal, he replied, "To get my wife back." After we discussed that this was not an appropriate counseling goal, we began to focus on what he could do to improve his situation.

Action Plan

1. **Take responsibility for your behavior.** Recognize your role in the situation. How did you contribute to the end result? What behaviors do you need to change? In what way is this your responsibility also? Be honest with yourself if you really want to change.

2. **Establish reasonable goals.** If your goal is not reasonable, what other outcomes would work to improve your circumstances? In other words, what will be the focus of therapy? In this case, we sought ways to improve his everyday reality. By working on his mental health, he could more clearly act in ways that might help him achieve more realistic goals.

3. **Examine your thoughts and perceptions, and change them if necessary.** Instead of thinking, "I am lonely," think, "I have more time to create what I have really wanted all along." Then figure out what this is. What is it that you really want?

4. **Change your behavior.** Do something different. What you have been doing thus far has not paid off. It is time to move forward with life and try out new behaviors. You can go out with a friend, reconnect with your loved ones, or find some new way to spend your time. It doesn't so much matter what you do, as long as you do something different.

5. **Work on soul qualities and practice empathy exercises.** Often men and women have trouble understanding each other, and what they want. Practicing soul qualities (see pages 49–51) and learning empathy are often initial steps toward understanding.

This man's issues ran deeper than can be expressed here, but this was our start. Even if you can't change your circumstances right now, you can make your personal reality a better place. You can learn to think in new ways and be open to new possibilities. You can create a better life for yourself. Once you are happier, the circumstances in your life will reflect your happiness. You can create change in your life.

10

There Is a Higher Power

While not all religions agree on what to call it, most agree that there is a power greater than ourselves operating in the world around us. My definition of the Higher Power is the overall spirit of all energy. In this respect, the words *God*, *Spirit*, and *Energy* can be used interchangeably. The Higher Power is a being of energy that is the sum of all energy. It is the "everything." Yet, as with any whole, it is greater than simply the sum of its parts. For example, our bodies are made up of a network of individual cells. While each cell is an entity or life form of its own, each is also part of a larger whole. Yet the whole, or the person in this case, is more than just a sum of cells. A life force within the self transcends the operations of the cells themselves. That life force, in fact, produces the operation of the cells. This is the energy that runs through all living things, from the amoeba to the genius, from the plant to the person. This is the Higher Power.

Different cultures may give different names to this Higher Power, but the definition of who or what it is remains the same. God or Buddha or Spirit or Allah signifies an energy that gives life to all life, and is wise beyond all of our reasoning.

This definition of God often conflicts with a more conventional religious definition, which sees God as a parent figure, or the Source from which all things are created. Let me illustrate this further.

God the Creator, or God the Father/Mother

God the Creator signifies that God is a parental figure; a father/mother figure who creates and then cares for his offspring. He created us in His image, and our goal is thus to please Him or at least attempt to follow in His footsteps. From this viewpoint, many believe that we are then rewarded for good deeds and thoughts and are punished for our sins. In this view, many people see God as a "boss" figure who controls all, and becomes vengeful when He is angered.

You may find it beneficial to think of God as a loving and supportive parent rather than a vengeful boss, especially if the latter image keeps you from feeling close to your God. Parents love their children for who they are. They may not agree with all of their decisions, and most likely would live their lives differently, but they love them still the same. Parents do what they can to help children find their own way. Parents understand that a child is a child, and that part of being a child is learning from your mistakes. We punish ourselves much more often than we are punished by anyone or anything else. In fact, we all have a judge inside of us, and we alone are responsible for our thoughts, words, and deeds.

God the Source

A different and somewhat less conventionally religious model of God is as the Source. In this model, God is the source of all energy that has ever existed or will ever exist. To illustrate this, think of God being to man as the sun is to the earth. Without the sun, there could not be life on earth. The sun supplies—unconditionally and without prejudice—energy and light to the whole earth, every second. There is never a lack of sun. It is always available. Sometimes there are clouds that block our view of the sun, but the sun is always there—shining on us through the clouds. At night, we rotate away from the sun, but its energy still wraps around us. The sun supplies light, energy, warmth, comfort, and *life*. We *must* have it to survive.

In this line of thought, God is nurturing and loving. The energy given out is constant and unconditional. A person's deeds or actions do not predict whether the sun will shine or not. *It is equally available to all.* You can't even refuse it if you want to. It is everywhere. You don't even have to accept this light for it to exist in your life and keep you alive.

From this example, it is easy to visualize God as a source of light and life in our lives. When we want more of this light, we can seek it by finding the sunshine (either mentally or literally) and basking in its light and warmth. When we want to hide away in shame and guilt, we find a dark place somewhere to cower and hide in fear. And though we may try to hide from it, the sun shines on us anyway—providing us warmth, encouraging growth, supplying what we need to survive, and keeping us alive. *This light shines equally on all and loves all unconditionally and without exception.* It is available to all and can be used for growth and healing. All you need do is seek it and you will find it.

Commonalities

In both models or definitions, God is the central or main figure in life. God is all things and yet more. This implies that God is both male and female and yet is neither. God is black and white and brown, yet cannot be identified as any one. God is all dualities and yet none of them. God is all there is.

God is both the Creator and the Source, the father and the mother, a guardian and a friend. God is light. God is unconditional love. God is life.

If you are uncomfortable with any of the words that I use, replace them with ones that suit your views. My goal is not to push religious doctrine, but to help you find your own brand of spirituality, and begin to define and experience that for yourself. To me, it is more a question of *morality* than religion. The decisions in life are based on an ultimate choice between "good" and "evil." And *good* is defined in your actions, words, and intentions.

Connecting with God or a Higher Power is an individual thing. The experience is unique for everyone. It is a process of opening your heart to love and learning how to have faith. It is a process of learning trust, and an acceptance that there is more to life than we know.

The church, or organized religion, is one path toward God; I do not believe it is the *only* path. The church can guide you and hopefully facilitate this feeling of oneness with God. But it is not the only ingredient in this recipe. Your individual experience with God is my focus here. How you choose to experience this is your decision. Whatever your individual view of God is, though, I encourage you to challenge it. Think about how you were raised to view God, and make sure that this view fits logically into your current view of reality.

Each religion has its own philosophy, and each believes that its way of thinking is the only "right" way. But how can all of these religions be "right" at the same time? How can any of us ever really know what is "right"? The answer is that there are no right or wrong answers. While we can philosophize for years on end about the way things are, no one can prove beyond a doubt that his way is the one and only correct way. The best you can do is find what is right for you.

Finding a place for quiet thinking, prayer, and relaxation in your daily life is good for your mental and spiritual health. Find time in your schedule to celebrate all that you have in your life, and just to be grateful and joyous. Appreciate the God that you have come to know, and know that wonderful things appear just when you need them most.

Part Three

Finding the Balance,
Creating the New

11

Integration

In Part One, we explored your personal reality—the reality that exists within you. You became more aware of your body, mind, and soul—your personal trinity. You also learned about the degree of control that you have over these three aspects of your self. And you began to use this information to shape your reality.

In Part Two, five general truths of shared reality were discussed and demonstrated. You learned the power of thought for the creation of your current state of mind. You learned how to talk to a wise part of yourself when you feel a need for reflection or a desire to gain insight. Reality around you became clearer.

Now, in Part Three, you'll learn to integrate your personal reality with shared reality. We'll explore how to find harmony and balance between what is going on inside you and what is happening all around you. You'll create something new and beautiful that is all yours: your own personal brand of reality.

In this way, you can figure out what you really want, and become open to the highest form in which it can come into your life; you can find congruence in your thoughts, actions, and feelings. All of your systems will work together toward the same goal, instead of fighting each other every step of the way. Ultimately, you'll learn how to change your thinking, change your behavior, and alter your emotions.

12

Living in Balance

Achieving Congruence

Congruence is the agreement between your internal feelings and thoughts and your actual experience of the world around you. When these two aspects are in congruence, they work together toward a common goal; when they are incongruent, they work against each other and cause problems internally. For example, you may perceive that you are a good employee. You come to work most days, and finish most work by the deadline. You try not to complain too much. In your mind, you are doing at least as much as most of your coworkers, and are equally as deserving as they are of raises and bonuses. Now, say your boss passes you up for a promotion and gives it to someone else. You confront your boss and ask why this happened, and your boss lists twenty reasons why this other person's work ethic is better than yours. In this case, there is incongruence between your perception of your work and your boss's perception.

In cognitive-behavioral terms, congruence must be obtained in three main areas for any plan to be successful:

- your thoughts and intentions;
- your behaviors and actions; and
- your emotions and feelings.

To accomplish any goal more quickly, align these three things. Align your thoughts with your actions with your feelings. Make sure that they are all working toward the same goal, and then make sure that this goal is worthy.

When your thoughts say that this is a good day, and your actions reflect this, and you feel good about it, then you are in congruence and having a good day. If your thoughts say that you are going to accomplish something, and you are working on doing so while thinking positive thoughts about its completion, then you have congruence and will accomplish your goal.

What Do You Want?

Perhaps the most important question you can continually ask yourself is, "What do I really want?" And perhaps the most important thing you can do for your mental health is to answer it honestly, completely, and from your heart.

What do you really want? A car? A better job? A relationship? A bigger house? Some other material thing? Think about that for a moment. What would having that thing do for you? What would it bring to you?

We don't often ask ourselves why we want something; we just know that we want it. Well, I am asking you now, "Why do you want that?" How would having it make you feel? What need or desire would be fulfilled by having it?

Underneath every wish is a desire for a feeling state that the realization of this wish is supposed to bring. A desire for wealth may stem from a desire for respect or power or freedom. A desire for a relationship may stem from a desire for connection, love, or sharing. A desire for a bigger house may symbolize a desire for expansion, growth, and/or breathing space.

Determine the factors that drive your desires, by examining your expectations of what those desires will bring. What is the essence of what you want? What need are you trying to fulfill? What are you craving?

As a society, we give great emotional importance to affluence. We admire and desire wealth and having things and getting more and more. We think that by having more we will be happy—that affluence will automatically solve all of our problems.

If this is true, why are there so many miserable rich people? And why do so many lottery winners divorce within two years of winning?

Money, affluence, and wealth are not the answers to life's problems. They couldn't be—they are too complicated. They take too much time to achieve, and as they solve some problems, they create others. People who have more generally spend more and do more. The more you obtain, the more effort you must expend to maintain all the things that you have obtained. The more you go and do, the less time you have for yourself, and the more complicated your life becomes.

There is no magic formula—not even money—that can take all your problems away and make you happy all the time. In fact, no *thing* can *make* you feel any particular way. *Circumstances* and *things* do not produce emotional states; people and their thoughts do.

So, if it's money you want, I encourage you to question your motives or intentions. What do you hope it will bring? If it is to get you out of debt, explore what being in debt feels like to you. This is such a common problem that I will expand on it here with a counseling session.

CS—*What do you want?*

MS—I want a hundred thousand dollars.

CS—*OK, what do you want it for?*

MS—I want it to pay off my bills, get out of debt, buy a better car, and take care of my family.

CS—*Tell me about how it feels to be in debt. Try to describe it in a picture, like a single-frame cartoon.*

MS—I feel tied down. Heavy. I feel like a can't ever do what I want to do, because so many people are wanting more and more, and I feel like I have less and less.

CS—*So the picture you see is yourself tied down?*

MS—Yes, I see ropes all around me tying me to all the sources of my debt. They are pulling and tugging on me and wanting more and more. It is getting harder for me to make it. There is so much holding me down.

CS—*You see your debts as ropes that tie you down, held by your creditors. They are pulling and tugging you in all directions, and this makes you feel insecure and unstable.*

Now, I want you to see yourself in this picture freeing yourself from these binds. Do this in whatever way feels right and let me know when you are done.

MS—I see myself giving each of them what they are asking for—paying off my debt. I see this as a ball of light going down each rope to the person or thing holding it at the other end. Each ball of light has all the money I owe and pays off what is owed in that relationship, and it releases its hold on me. I see myself being released from each burden as they let go and move away from me. The balls of light continue to shoot down each rope until all the ropes are free.

CS—*How does this feel in comparison to the previous picture?*

MS—It feels much better, lighter, and freer. I feel more in balance with the other person. They do not have so much power over me. I feel more on level ground.

CS—*So, perhaps what you are most concerned about in your debt is a feeling of inferiority or imbalance—of being less than or being tied to someone else who has more.*

MS—I guess underneath it probably feels that way. But what I feel more now is that when I have debt, I have fewer choices and am more limited. I also feel somewhat insecure about my ability to fulfill my end of these obligations. Money may not bring happiness, but it certainly can make life more fun. And it does seem to bring more options.

CS—*Yes, you are right. When used wisely, money can serve you and bring more beauty and options into your life. Yet there are usually other things that can fulfill you in the same ways that money does. Love and friendships and relationships are the prime examples of this. When you have valuable relationships you have perhaps the greatest gift of all. And relationship is what your image seems to be all about. The imbalance in relationship between money you owe and money you have.*

MS—Yes, balance and relationships are both big things for me.

CS—*Balance is what you can focus on now. Seek balance in your thoughts and your actions involving money. Make a plan to pay off each rope, one at a time, and trust that you are going to make it through. Get financial advice if you need it, but begin to get this area in balance. And try to remember that each entity or person would not have loaned you money if they thought you would not pay them back. They had enough faith in you to lend to you. You can have faith enough in yourself to prove them correct in their assumption.*

MS—OK. I have something I can focus on now—an image that I can re-create and adapt as time goes on. I am beginning to see myself actually doing this. I can feel the emotions coming more into balance.

CS—*Well, that is enough for now. Any time you find yourself worrying about money or debt, imagine a picture of you solving the problem and watch it happen. Use the imagery to find creative solutions to your problems.*

For review, here are the questions to examine:
1. What do you want?
2. What will that bring you?
3. What do you *really* want?

I encourage you to ask yourself these questions often. After finding the emotional state that you desire, seek to fulfill that state of mind in some way other than by owning some item. Items rarely last, anyway; emotional states are renewable. You don't have to go shopping to find them; you just have to look within. You don't have to wait for a sale—they are available to you anytime you seek them. They cost nothing to obtain, and they take up no space in your house.

Exercise: Creating a Desired Emotional State

If you are seeking a particular emotional state from an item or circumstance, decide now that you can find that emotional state without having the object or circumstance.

Choose one emotional state that you would like to inhabit. For this example, I will use *security*, a common desire. Security, or the need to feel secure, underlies many things and is essential for basic mental health.

To start, get an image—like a single-frame cartoon—of what *security* feels like and looks like to you. This may be difficult at first, but it is important, so continue to try. If you have trouble finding an image, begin examining what the word or concept means to you. How do you feel when you feel secure? What does feeling secure bring? At what times in your life do you seek security most?

The image I get when working with *security* is me standing on solid ground—immovable, strong, solid ground beneath my feet. I often see this as a thick, wide rock that appears indestructible. I see myself standing firmly and proudly on this rock. Nothing is shifting beneath my feet. This is solid ground. I am standing straight and tall with my feet firmly planted.

Your image may be very different, and that is fine. There are no "right" or "wrong" images. What you see is symbolic for you.

Maintain this image until you feel the way you want to feel. Recognize that you can create your state of mind with focused concentration on that which you want to create.

Alternate Exercise: Creating a Desired Emotional State

Many times, the mind interferes with the creation of an image, so another way to create an emotional state is to focus intently on that state of mind.

Take a few minutes to breathe deeply and relax. Focus on the word that symbolizes the state of mind you are looking for. For example, if you are seeking peace, focus on the word *peace*. Repeat it in your mind over and over, and clear your thoughts from anything other than peace. As you repeat "peace" as a mantra, allow your mind to associate freely about what peace means to you. Follow your thoughts and allow them to create images, sounds, feelings, emotions, and so on, related to peace and the experience of peace. Stay in this place of peace for as long as you desire. When you feel satisfied and peaceful, you can switch to focusing on another emotion/feeling state, or you can return to normal awareness.

Establishing Priorities

Often, when I ask the question, "What do you want?" the answer is a laundry list of wishes that have been saved up for some time. The answer gets longer and longer as you dream about all that you want. This is good and productive, in that it helps you see all the things that you want; at some point, however, priority must be established.

What do you want the most? What do you want to work on establishing first? What will bring you the greatest reward? These are all questions to help establish priority. Some general guidelines might be helpful here.

- It is more productive for the goal to be a feeling state or essence than a particular material object or circumstance.
- It is more beneficial to aim for something with the proviso that it be "best for everyone involved." In other words, your goal should not be to the detriment of others, or cause harm to others in any way.
- Think forward and upward. Aim for the highest and brightest path available.
- Recognize that priorities may change daily, so reassess them often.
- Be clear in your thinking. Know what you want.
- Keep your goals and the essence of your goals in the present tense.
- Be careful what you ask for, because you just might get it!

Loving, Supportive Relationships

For years, I have been asking myself, "What do I want?" as a continual exercise in creating and re-creating my reality, as a method for testing out theories, as a way to sample various paths, and as a way to remind myself of what I am doing. I have found that I can easily create material things. They do not always come in the form that I expect them to, and they often do not live up to other expectations, but I usually do get whatever it was I asked for—eventually. Yet, while I have these things in my life, I find that they generally do not fulfill me. As much as I *love* material things (and shopping for them), having them still never really satisfies what I am craving.

A few years ago, it finally occurred to me that material things might not be what I wanted after all. I was a recently divorced single mom, working two jobs. I had a private practice doing counseling several hours a week, on top of a forty-hour work week at my "real" job. Much of my identity had been tied up in my first marriage. With my education and background (and my experience leading a divorce workshop in the past) I was probably better equipped than most to deal with all the identity issues that came with my divorce. While devastating at times, it was also extremely liberating at others. Here I was, thirty years old, trying to figure out *yet again* who I was and what I was looking for in life—except that this time, I could choose anything I wanted. It was all up to me. There was no one else to blame if I made the "wrong" decisions. I had to take responsibility for what I might next bring into my life. And I was bound and determined that it would not be the same kinds of circumstances that had led me to where I was at that stage—stunned and alone.

As I began to date and explore what other relationships might bring, I asked myself continually, "What do I want?" I repeatedly came up with the same few themes—companionship, support (of all kinds—emotional, mental, physical, and financial), and, most of all, love. I wanted to have equal partners in all my relationships. And I wanted support in all of my relationships, because most of what I do is support others. Thus, I created a phrase that became a mantra for finding the perfect relationship. In my definition, perfect relationships are *loving, supportive relationships.*

I found quickly that this formula generalized to friends and colleagues as well as to love interests. To my pleasant surprise, my friends came out of the woodwork to help me in whatever ways they could. My two closest friends offered routine babysitting for my three-year-old, so I could continue my private practice two evenings a week—something I would not have been able to do without their help. My mother, living three hours away, offered assistance in all the ways that she could. People began helping me, as I had helped them so many times before. It was incredible to feel and know this level of support in my life. Finally, I was feeling something that was fulfilling. Finally, I was creating something that was worthwhile to have. Thus, my mantra gained momentum. I would not get into a love relationship again if it did not meet my needs in this way. In all of my relationships from this point forward, I would seek a balance in support, from a basis of love. This became the minimal requirement of any relationship I would enter into ever again.

Thus, we get to the topic of *loving, supportive relationships.* In my experience with other people, as well as with myself, I have found this to be an incredible gift. If you are in a relationship that has a basis of love or loving support, and there is a reciprocal giving and receiving cycle involved, this becomes a healthy relationship. Where there is support for each other in admiration and love, there is balance and kindness and health.

Supporting one another is a tremendous gift, even if it is just emotional support. Add in a little physical support (a carpool group, help with bigger projects, and so on), and life gets even nicer. Mix in love, and life is grand.

I have found more and more that when we have each other, we have all that we need. The size of your income has little significance when compared to the amount of support you have. Being in loving, supportive relationships takes you so much further than your paycheck, which most likely barely helps you make it through the month. The people in our lives are what matter, not the things. And while I have always known this on a mental level, I had to experience it firsthand.

So, you *can* create anything you want. You can obtain any and all of your material desires. But, let me save you some time (and a few years of practice): work on your relationships first. These are the people who walk through life with you. These people will be there even when you have nothing. This is where you will get the love that you desire and the support that you need. You will love and support them in return.

13

Taking Control of What You Can

Once you have figured out what you can and cannot control, and what you do and do not want, then you can begin to put these ideas into action.

The key to this plan is the revision process. Life is never finished; it is always in revision. Circumstances change, feelings change, people change their minds—nothing stays the same. When a working plan suddenly stops working, the obvious choice is to modify it. When a plan is still working but your position changes or your feelings change somehow, a modification might be a good idea.

Let's review the necessary steps for taking control.

Know What You Can and Cannot Control

What you can control	What you cannot control
Your emotions	Other people
Your behaviors	The past
Your circumstances	Your family of origin

What you can control	What you cannot control
Your mind/thoughts/ decisions	Your birth order/position in family
Your bodily appearance (to an extent)	Your biology/chemistry
Your personal future	Global circumstances (to an extent)
Your perceptions	Other people's perceptions

Know What You Do and Do Not Want

Ask yourself: *Is this really what I want? What will this bring me when I have it? How will things be different if I have it? Do I want that? Is there another way I can get that same feeling? What do I really want—that feeling or that thing?*

Follow your train of thought, and gently keep it on track. If you do not know what you want, how are you going to recognize it when you have it? Remember, you do not have to know exactly what you want in terms of material or physical things, but you do need to know what you want to feel and experience on an emotional and mental level.

Own Only What Is Yours

If someone close to you is in a bad mood, but you are in a good mood, do not let that other person give you her bad mood—even if she tries really hard to spread it. Own only your feelings, thoughts, and perceptions. Accept into your belief system only those beliefs and ideas that resonate with you.

This idea is especially important when you are dealing with someone who is angry, pouty, or just plain mean. It can be difficult not to reflect those traits if you are around a person like this frequently, yet you still do have control. So, here are some pointers for dealing with difficult people displaying difficult emotions.

1. Accept that this feeling state belongs to that person—*not to you.* You do not have to join her in this desolate place. It will not do either of you any good. It will only contribute to the problem at an energy level, for you are feeding that energy even more and allowing it to come further into your life. Stand your ground, and stay disconnected from the emotion.

2. If you are trying to help this person to settle down from her strong feelings, then listening to the content—without taking on the emotion—is OK. Listen, from a detached point of view, to what she is upset about.

3. Now that you are listening to the content in a detached kind of way, what do you hear? What is she really communicating? What is underneath her anger? Fear or worry is probably somewhere underneath her anger. The underlying emotion needs to be addressed.

4. Find a way to gently point out the underlying emotions. You might say something like, "I hear what you are saying and I understand where you are coming from, but let's try to look at this objectively." Restate the issue from an outsider's objective view, and see if this rational approach helps her. Then add, "I understand why this makes you angry, but is this anger doing you any good? It is obviously bad for your health and mental state. Maybe there is a more productive feeling we can generate from this." From this point, you can make a plan for changing things for the better or determine how to deal with the problem in some other way. It may be that you cannot do anything to help her change the situation. In that case, begin to look at it in a different way that won't cause daily discomfort.

Remember that chronically angry people are probably dealing with other mental health issues like depression or low self-esteem.

While this does not justify their behavior in any way, it does explain it somewhat. If you can deal with the root cause—the depression, the lower feelings of self-worth, the feelings of being trapped or out of control—then you will make much more progress than if you simply deal with the emotional outburst at hand. If you are not qualified to help this person, you may need to find outside help.

Learn to Keep an Open Mind

Open-minded thinking is one of the greatest gifts that you can give yourself, and it is particularly important in today's society. We do not always know the answer to every question, and we may not ever learn some of the answers. Open your mind to accept that there may be more to this than you know. Have faith that a force of love is operating to assist all who seek it. Believe that you will know what you need to know when you need to know it. Trust your intuitions and act on them.

You do not have to be "right" all the time to be a valuable person. Your worth is not defined by your intelligence. However, if you are unwilling to learn or explore new and different ideas, then you are severely limiting your thinking and your ability to create new ideas.

Open your mind to the possibility that more exists than you are currently aware of. Recognize that you might not have all the answers just yet. Never stop asking the questions. Keep an open mind and you will find what you are looking for.

Work on Your Defensiveness

If you find that you are reacting defensively to others more often than not, this is a clue that there is something you need to look at closely in your life. You may feel that in some way your rights are being violated or something is not fair. Maybe you are reacting to a feeling or sense, and not just to words. You may be feeling fear on some level. Whatever the reason, explore it even deeper. What is it that you are really reacting to? What bothers you so much that you would allow your body to work itself up into this state? Why does this affect you so much?

Only you can answer those questions for yourself, and you cannot stop reacting defensively until you do.

Exercise: Dealing With Defensiveness

Get an image in your mind of a situation in which you are reacting defensively. Imagine the situation in as much detail as you can. What is happening in your picture? What are you reacting to, and what is your reaction? What is your facial expression? Your body language? What else do you notice about yourself?

Next, see yourself stepping out of this situation and examining it from another point of view. Stand back from a more objective place, and look at the whole picture with everyone else included.

Continue to acknowledge that this thing or person did upset you, but recognize this from a more detached point of view. Think about it more logically. Why did it upset you? Was this person trying to get a reaction? If she was and you gave it to her, then didn't she win? What is really going on here? Is there some other way you could react that might produce a healthier result? Is there some action that can be taken to improve this situation?

Examine the situation from as many angles as you like. Put yourself in the other person's shoes. See yourself from a friend's view. See the situation from a higher place within yourself. What is different about it now? What is the lesson in this? If we can get the lesson this time, we won't have to repeat it over and over again. This scenario is really getting old. It is so time to move on.

Now, rewind your mental tape and replay the original scene, but this time, instead of reacting defensively, react in some other way. You have a chance to try something different. How would it be different this time? Or would it?

You can play out any number of scenarios. You can try several different approaches and compare the reactions. While it is all in your mind, it prepares you for various situations and gives you a chance to figure them out. You can make mistakes in your own reality and learn from them, so you do not have to repeat them in the shared reality.

Stop Allowing Others to Push Your Buttons

People can upset you only if you let them. You can take the long route and analyze every situation that arises in your life, or you can learn to avoid these situations altogether. By using visualization techniques combined with cognitive-behavioral therapy, you can stop allowing others to push your emotional buttons. They may still push, but you will not react. You are finished playing that game. You have risen above that situation and have seen it for what it truly is.

Following are some additional visual images you can use to reduce the effects that other people's energies have on you. You can use these images anywhere, at any time. They are most effective when combined with positive self-talk. Become your counselor self, and talk yourself through this and any other situation.

Guided Imagery Exercises

Someone has sent negative energy in your direction (such as anger or hate). You can respond in any of the following ways:

The Fan. See an imaginary fan in front of you. Mentally turn the fan on and stand in front of it. The air blows any negative energy away. The wind is powerful and cleansing.

The Breeze. This is a more gentle version of the fan. Simply feel a breeze blow the negative feelings past you. What you do not want from this other person cannot attack you. It is being gently carried away from you on the breeze.

The Waterfall. Someone has invaded your space, and you desperately want to cleanse that energy from inside and around you. See and feel yourself standing under a beautiful waterfall. The waterfall cleanses you—inside and out. It is incredible to feel this energy wash through you. You are cleansed in the water and in the light. You are protected and safe.

The Bubble. Imagine yourself in a clear bubble. The bubble extends above and below you and surrounds you on all sides. This bubble is made of an incredible material that you control. The porous aspect of the bubble allows in any energy you wish to enter. But the elastic aspect of the bubble closes on demand, and bounces away any energy you do not like. If something comes your way that you do not wish to take on, simply close your bubble and watch it bounce away. It can either bounce back to the person or thing who sent it, or better yet, you can bounce it to the Universal Recycling Center to be recycled into light.

Become Transparent. In this image, simply become invisible to those energies that you do not like, and you will feel less of their effect on you. They pass right by you or through you. They never try to take hold because they don't have anything to take hold of. They do not even recognize you because you are transparent to them. This is often the most difficult exercise for one to do completely. You may have to evolve with practice on this one. Just think *transparent*, and hold that energy. It will hold longer with time.

Redirect Your Thoughts

If you find yourself thinking something that you do not want to think, simply redirect your thoughts to something different. Remind yourself to breathe fully, wipe the slate clean, and decide to think something different.

Example: You find yourself thinking that you are never going to make some deadline, or get something done. You begin to feel frazzled, and the more frazzled you become, the harder it is to focus on accomplishing your goal. Your mind gets all fuzzy, and you finally catch yourself mid-thought. You realize that you are only confusing matters, and you decide to get a grip. You take a deep breath, think of a calming color, breathe again, and clear your mind. Once you are in a focused place, you go through, in your mind, the steps you need to take to accomplish your goal. Calmly write them down. You begin to see a list of priorities emerging, and you number these tasks from most urgent to least. You gain control over the chaos in your mind. You win. Your mind wins, for now it has a plan, and your actions can now be deliberate and purposeful. You have redirected your thoughts. You have control.

Taking control of your thoughts is truly this easy. You are the only one who can dictate what you think. This is the one area you can truly control. It is time to start controlling it.

14

Recognizing and Interpreting Personal Messages

What are personal messages? Personal messages are signals—sent by your wiser self, your subconscious, or the universe—that tell you that you need to look at something. These entities are constantly sending you messages, trying to get you to listen, but you often miss or dismiss these events or symbols as coincidences or bizarre happenings. Learn to recognize certain signals and their meanings. Learn to see the symbolism in your life.

Ways in Which You Receive Messages

Bodily Signals

The body responds at a physical level to everything around you. If it tenses up, what is it trying to say? By learning to recognize your bodily signals, you can better gauge your reactions to things. When you become aware of what is normal for you, you will more easily recognize when something is abnormal. Repeated bodily signals (appearing daily, or several times per week) require attention as well. If every time you eat a certain food, you puff up and become miserable for hours, then perhaps it is time to consider if this is the right food for you. If every time you are around a certain person you get a headache, you might examine your relationship with and reactions to this person.

Repeated Thoughts

If thoughts keep recurring and running through your head, stop and consider them. What are they trying to tell you? What is the message? Why does this theme keep coming back to you? What is really going on?

Urgings

Unexplained urgings to do something or say something often have a message. Listen to your intuition if it is telling you to do something. Perhaps there is something you need to know or do. Trust in this if it feels right and good.

Things Appearing out of the Blue

If something good finds you, accept it graciously and gratefully. It is there for some reason. You may not know what the reason is just now, but you can rest assured that if it is there, it is supposed to be.

Synchronicities

"Coincidences" do not happen by chance; they are part of the grander design. Sometimes things happen just as they are supposed to. See the patterns and the messages in life all around you, because they are there for a reason.

Dreams (Recurrent, Vibrant, or Bizarre)

Some dreams stand out in your mind for a reason. They are particularly vivid or bright or realistic. These dreams are trying to convey something to you. Listen for the meaning in the symbols.

Because dreams can be fascinating, and are such a constant part of our lives, let us consider them even further.

Dreams are your brain's way of talking to you when you are sleeping. Your brain never goes to sleep. It never stops thinking and examining and pondering. It never stops sending signals to your heart to keep beating, and to your lungs to keep breathing. Yet, while your brain may not need sleep, your body very much needs physical rest. When your body has had all it can take and goes to sleep, your brain is still active. Perhaps this is when your brain (and possibly your soul) sees you as an active listener, and begins to talk to you in ways that it hopes you will understand.

Some nights your dreams may just be "brain chatter"—a replaying of events that happened in the recent past, or of some commentary that you've had going on inside your mind for some time. Other nights, your brain (or soul) may have a story to tell you. On these nights, you have a storylike dream that feels unusual, bizarre, or in some way stands out as important. These dreams are the ones that you should examine. Whether they are good dreams or nightmares, they may contain a wealth of symbols and hidden messages that your subconscious will not entertain in waking reality. The only way your subconscious can entertain these ideas is through your dreams.

If this is true, if your dreams are your brain's way of talking to you while you sleep, then how might the brain speak to you in a way you that you can understand? The easiest way to convey a whole concept or idea in a short and definite way is through a symbol. Instead of the brain trying to spell out "danger" to you, it might send a symbol that represents "danger"—like a big, ugly monster, or a dangerous situation, or a stop sign, or a rattle in the car in your dream that may symbolize a significant mechanical malfunction. These are all ways that your brain can communicate a larger amount of information in a single image or object.

Even if you don't consider yourself a "visual" person, your mind still does dream—it just perceives the dream in some other form. We use any or all of our senses to perceive the messages in a dream. Think about your dreams: in an elaborate and vivid dream, you may see the story unfolding, hear the noises all around you, sense the danger or the emotion, smell familiar smells, or taste the flavors presented. You can use all of your senses in dreams, just as you can in waking reality. In fact, the more senses that are used in the dream, the more elaborate and complete the dream becomes. The more elaborate the dream is, the more likely it is to have some meaning that you can then decipher upon awakening.

Because you are dreaming the dream in your mind, and your mind has created the symbols and the meanings that they will have to you, you are the only one who can interpret and decipher these symbols. The best way to begin to decipher your mind's messages is through a dream journal. As soon as you can upon awakening, write down those dreams that stand out in your mind as important. Write down every detail that you can remember, and note what stands out in the dream as any form of emotional reaction. If you were scared, if you were concerned or frightened, note that. Not every single object is going to be symbolic, but note whatever seems significant to you.

The following exercise can help you remember your dreams. The more you get into the habit of doing this, the more easily you will remember what you have dreamed.

Exercise: Dream Journal

Write down a dream in as vivid detail as possible. Include color and contrasts, and describe feelings, emotions, and perceptions from the dream. If it was strange, how was it strange? If your dream was telling you a story, what was the story? Did it have a beginning, middle, and end? Did it have a purpose or define a path? Did it have a conclusion or answer? What did it mean to you?

Writing down the dream in detail is therapeutic in and of itself. Often, just in the act of writing it down, the dream analyzes itself. You see the symbolism as you describe it on paper. You see it from a different angle and perspective. You recognize your feelings and reactions to things within the dream, and see the symbolism in these reactions.

If you have written down the dream in vivid detail and still have no idea what it means, then begin to examine various aspects of the dream. Pick one or two symbols or objects in the dream that stand out in your mind, and examine these symbols. Say, for example, that throughout the dream, a bird flies by repeatedly. What kind of bird is it? Does that bird mean anything to you or have any special significance in your life? Is there a time in the dream when the bird appears especially often? What color is the bird? Is there anything about its flight that seems unusual? Is there a feeling that you have as the bird flies by?

Your emotional reaction to something in a dream is often what is important. You may see a plain white house or flower in a dream, but that image stays with you the whole day because it stood out in the dream for some reason. If this is the case, examine the emotional response as well as the symbol itself. The house or flower itself may not be familiar, but the feeling it invokes in the dream may be significant.

Even if you remember only images from a dream rather than a sequence of events, those flashes can be just as valuable. Each flash may contain a message that is trying to be conveyed.

Think back to a recent dream. Recall an image, feeling, sensation, or picture of the dream, and make this image or sensation as detailed as you can. What is happening? Is there action? Or is it a still picture? What are the feelings or emotions involved? (The absence of feelings is significant too.) Do any colors or symbols stand out in the image? Who else was there? Were you seeing this image from afar, or were you part of the action, looking through your own eyes? Is there any message or feeling you get from the dream? Was there a sense of anything that seems important to you?

Recurrent Dreams

Recurrent dreams are important because the symbolism keeps repeating itself, as if trying to get your attention. Whether you have the dream twice, or every night for a week, something is significant or you wouldn't be dreaming it over and over again. Write down these dreams, even if they are unpleasant, and examine what the dream might be telling you. If you have no idea what a symbol might mean, it is OK to look it up in a dream dictionary. Just beware that someone else's definition may or may not fit your experience or ideas. It is also a good idea to look at symbolism specifically in terms of repetition: if you have a recurrent dream in which you are abandoned, abandonment issues are what you need to look at—not necessarily just how you were abandoned in the dream.

Nightmares and Unpleasant Dreams

With people who frequently have nightmares, I have noticed patterns to the action sequences in their dreams. They may not always have the same dream, but an action sequence seems similar throughout the dreams. For example, they are always being chased by something scary, or they are always in a dangerous situation trying to figure out how to get out or stay alive. The themes are what seem to be significant about these dreams.

If you have nightmares or scary dreams, look for patterns in the action that takes place. Are you always defending yourself in some way? Are you always running from something? Are you always at the mercy of something larger than yourself? Notice your position or the role that you play in the dream, and how the dream ends. Are you a fighter in the dream, or do you run and hide? Does the dream end with you beating the bad thing or winning? Or does it end before a conclusion occurs? These aspects of the dream are just as important as the content itself.

If you do notice a pattern in your dreams, consider if this is symbolic of something happening in your waking reality. If it is, attempt to address this pattern in your waking reality, and notice if your dreams change as a result.

Example: Dream Interpretation of a Recurrent Nightmare

The Dream. A storm is coming. A woman hears the weather alerts, but she doesn't know where the sound is coming from. She finds herself in a field beside her office, holding her infant son in her arms and running. They are out in the open with the storm coming. She suddenly knows that there is a tornado very close. She sees it in the sky over the trees. It is coming right toward them, and she is not sure where to go. She wants desperately to protect her son; she must find a way to keep him safe. She suddenly finds a shelter and gets inside. It seems like one other person, a man, is in the shelter with them. He was there before they got there. The tornado is overhead. The winds are blowing like crazy now, and the sound is incredible. She covers her son the best that she can. The tornado passes right over them and keeps moving. They make it through. She wakes up from the dream.

Outside Interpretation. This tells me that the woman is capable and confident. She was worried about the storm and keeping her son safe, but she remained calm. Safety appeared when she needed it most, and they were safe—despite the vicious danger overhead. She had faith that everything would be OK, and it was.

Dreamer's Interpretation. The dreamer couldn't help but wonder if the dream was prophetic. She had never dreamed about tornadoes before, and she rarely had recurring dreams. What was so important about the tornado? What danger could that represent? A few months after having these dreams, she found out that her husband was having an affair. The storm that followed was certainly intense, but she made it through, protecting her son as much as she could throughout. She found shelter and prayed that it would pass over. All worked out for the best in the end. They were safe.

At certain times in our lives, dreaming—both nighttime and day dreaming—may take on more importance than at others. Have you ever noticed that some periods of your life are filled with active dreaming, and at other times, you seem not to dream at all? Why is that? If dreaming is something our mind does all the time, why is that we only remember our dreams some times and not others?

Studies have shown that dreaming is not transient. We dream any time that we are in a state of rapid eye movement at night. Thus, if we are sleeping as we should, we are dreaming. Yet, only at certain periods in our lives are these dreams memorable, realistic, vivid, and/or meaningful.

Our awareness of the dreaming is transient—not the dreaming itself. Again, we may not know for sure why this is true, but it appears to have significance. My theory is that if you are remembering your dreams in vivid detail, perhaps there is a reason for this that you can examine. Likewise, there may be a reason that you cannot remember your dreams for some period of your life. As with all of life, go with the flow. Seek to understand, and you will likely be guided toward understanding. Accept that it might not be time to know, and then be open to the time when you can know. Be open to new possibilities.

No matter which dream you are examining, recognize your control and influence on it. If our dreams are mirrors of our thoughts, what are we thinking about that could induce these dreams? All types of dreams contain messages. Your job is to figure them out.

If you would like more information on this fascinating topic, I encourage you to read books and scientific journals on dreams and dream studies.

Symbols

Symbols are unique, in that different people perceive them in slightly different ways. Everyone's perception of reality is individual and unique; therefore, the definitions and meanings people give to things are individual and unique. At the same time, commonly held beliefs and ideas are related to certain symbols.

For example, take the cross. While we may each perceive the cross in a different way (we think different thoughts and experience unique feelings), we also know that the cross is a symbol of Christianity and the life of Jesus. So, while we all feel differently about it, the basic idea—the symbolism—is shared.

Pay attention to your perceptions of a symbol. If you see a cross in a dream or daydream, ask yourself what a cross means to you. Ask yourself how that is symbolic in your life, in your current circumstances. Just follow your train of thought and see where it takes you.

Common Symbols

The following list contains a few examples that can help you to define symbols for yourself. While they seem to be universally symbolic, I encourage you to define things for yourself. Ask yourself what each symbol or object means to you. If it means nothing, dismiss it and let it go. If it keeps coming back, there might be another message.

Air—light, flowing energy that sustains life

Angels—salvation, hope, miracles

Bread—life, body, nourishment

Breath (note the type and depth of the breath)—life and sustenance, relaxation and depth

Butterfly or flying insect—wings of flight, freedom, beauty, softness, gentleness, love, bringing of life (as a pollinator)

Chocolate—decadence, smoothness, joy, sharing, pleasure

Church—worship, communion, relationship, tradition, issues of guilt and retribution

Clock—passage of time, telling of time

Cross—Christianity, remembrance of Jesus, protection

Crystal—cleansing and transmuting energy

Dawn—new beginnings, a fresh start, another opportunity

Dove—peace, serenity, beauty

Earth—groundedness, nourishment, growth, home

Fairies, gnomes, little folk—playful and fun energy, tending to the environment, care of the earth, mischievous behavior, joy and thanksgiving, celebration, fantasy

Fire—energy, growth, burning desire, spirit

Fish—life, Christianity, sustenance

Flower—blooming, opening to the sunshine, growth, beauty

Heart—love, support, bringing and sustaining of life

House—habitation, embodiment, shelter, warmth, comfort, security, balance, sharing

Lighthouse—hope, shelter from storm, assistance, history, strength

Phone, computer—communication, information

Pot of gold—riches, luck, serendipity

Rainbow—hope, joy, beauty, fleeting moments, pot of gold at the end

Ring—loyalty, connection, neverending circle

Rock—solidity, stability, the Earth, permanence

Rose—passion, love, beauty, grace, delicacy, intoxicating fragrance

School—education, learning, early socialization

Storms (note type and duration of storm)—clashing systems, chaos, turmoil, fear, uncertainty, power

Sunset—an ending, beautiful colors, the fading of the day

Sunshine—light, growth, fire, heat, glow

Tree—solid wisdom that is both rooted in the ground and reaching into the sky; protection, life

Two people holding hands or embracing—relationship, support, love, companionship, mutual respect and admiration

Water (note the type and body of the water)—emotion, creation, movement, an obstacle to overcome, a feeling related to the behavior of the water (stillness, rushing, babbling, waves crashing)

Wind—free-flowing movement, gentle cleansing

Create Your Own Symbols

As previously stated, symbols have personal meanings as well as generalized meanings; therefore, it is easy for you to learn how to use symbols. You can never go wrong using a particular meaning for a symbol, because there are no "wrong" ways to perceive it.

Any time that you get an image, discover what it means to you. Say, for example, that you get an image of a white bird sitting on a thin brown branch, sinking its teeth into a ripe red cherry. Depending on the person having this image, it could mean several different things. One person might say that the white bird eating the red cherry is significant of purity and light over-indulging in earthly pleasures. The thin branch may symbolize the unstable nature of the experience. To another person, this is a vision of celebration and pleasure. The bird is partaking in a joyous reward and is rightfully savoring the experience.

What distinguishes these two interpretations is the feeling associated with the picture. In the first, the feeling is of indulgence and pride; in the second, the feeling is of joyous celebration. One person does not feel so comfortable with the image; the other delights in it.

The picture is the same no matter who sees it, yet each interprets it in her own way. Because we don't define things in absolutes on this planet, much of what is around us is there by interpretation only. While we agree on the meaning of some images, we also define images for ourselves.

As an exercise in mental health, I encourage you to play with images and symbols—especially the positive and uplifting ones. Create symbols and pictures in your mind of desirable states for yourself. If you recognize that you need a certain feeling—like appreciation or love—look inside and ask yourself what that looks like. Get an image or a feeling of what that is for you. Experience that inside for a moment, using this image. Then draw upon this image any time you want to feel that emotion or feeling.

In doing this, you are teaching yourself stimulus-response conditioning. You see the image (stimulus), and you have a desired response. You are training yourself to feel better about things. You are creating new pathways for normal response.

Symbols are important because they tend to create; you can learn to create with them. My only caution would be to remember that you must take responsibility for all of your actions. You must be aware of what you are doing at all times, and make sure that your motivations and intentions are pure love and light—the highest, brightest path for everyone involved.

15

Staying Mentally Healthy

Coping Skills 101

Coping skills are techniques that we use every day, as little reminders to ourselves that we are going to survive. They are our mantras, our affirmations, and the positive voices inside our heads that keep us looking forward and upward. Developing your own unique set of coping skills and defining your own coping style can be fun, and is certainly creative. To spark your imagination, try a few of the following ideas. If one of them doesn't suit you, be open to others that do.

Effective Coping Skills

Personalize these examples as you see fit.
1. *Practice the skills that you have learned in this book.*
   - Monitor your thoughts, and redirect the ones that need redirecting.
   - Be thankful and aware of all you have. Appreciate all you have, for there have certainly been times when you had less.

- Imagine desired results, and determine if these results are truly desirable. Define "desirable" to yourself, and redefine it often.
- Figure out what it is that you really want, and then have faith that, on some level, you already have it.
- Don't allow the chatter of the mind to control any part of you; on the contrary, take complete control of your mind. No one is controlling you; you are controlling yourself. Be a big kid, and take responsibility for that. The alternative is not an option in any case.

2. *Make an attempt to work through your problems.*

It doesn't much matter who you talk to about your problems, as long as you are talking about them. In a perfect world, this person would have your best interests at heart, and would guide you in the path of light without overly influencing your behavior. A teacher lights the path, but the student still has to walk it. Learning still must occur. There are several ways that you can talk through an issue, either with yourself or with another person.

- *Write in a journal.* Writing in a journal is a wonderful way to stay in touch with your thoughts and emotions. The more you write, the more you become aware of how you think and what you feel. You can write about anything and everything. A standard format that I recommend is to write down your dreams, followed by anything significant going on in your life, followed by your intentions for the day. Think of this as a "past, present, future" model for the morning or daily journal session. Writing your prayers and what you are thankful for are other forms of journaling activity.
- *Share with a loved one.* If you have someone in your life who you can talk to and trust, turn to this person when you need to work something out. Ask for another per-

spective, and be open to what that other perspective might show you. Recognize that all the sides of a story are its different perspectives. Realize that there might be more than one right answer. Be open to finding a solution that is good for everyone involved.

- *Seek professional help, if needed.* When you need someone who is not part of your life to give you a fresh perspective and/or new direction, seek the help of a professional counselor or therapist. The counselor's role is to get you focused on a path of healing. Your job is to walk that path. Do not expect your counselor to do it for you. Only you can do it for yourself. But, if you need the guidance, there are many who are qualified to show you the way.

3. *Learn how to relax, and do it often.*

Relaxation and downtime are especially important in today's hectic society. Part of being mentally healthy is knowing when you need to take time for yourself, and then being able to do it. Everyone develops her own style of relaxing, but here are some suggestions that might spark your imagination.

- *Listen to music.* Music can be incredibly therapeutic. Feelings and words that are expressed in music can touch you at an emotional level. Your mood will most likely dictate the type of music you listen to and when, but this is the beauty of music—you always have a wide variety to choose from. You can even use music to help create a certain mood or emotion. If you are feeling sad and listen to upbeat and happy music, you can often bring your emotions out of sadness and into a more joyful place. If you want to revel in your misery, you can always find an artist working through his misery in his music. Music allows you to relate to the artistry that the musician is expressing. It becomes intimate and expressive in this way.

- *Write it down.* Writing about what is going on inside your mind is a wonderful way to focus all of those stray and unfocused thoughts. You do not have to keep what you write, as in a formal journal, but it is often therapeutic to write it anyway. When you write, you must finish one sentence before you start the next. This discipline allows you to finish thoughts, instead of simply allowing them to wander around in your brain, over and over, with no goal or purpose. Once the writing begins to flow, you can often work through whatever problem or difficulty you are experiencing. You become more in touch with your emotions and thoughts about the issues, and can gain more clarity about what to do.
- *Take a warm bath.* Pampering yourself with a long hot soak in the tub is one way to treat yourself to a time and space for relaxation and peace. Allow the water to caress and comfort you. Enjoy the sensations of warmth and gentle healing. Clear your mind and enjoy the quiet moments. Then, when the time has come to get out of the tub, release the plug and allow all of your troubles to disappear down the drain for recycling.
- *Set the atmosphere.* Your surroundings influence your moods, so when you want to relax and unwind, one way to begin is to set the atmosphere around you to induce relaxation. You might light candles, turn down lights, put on soft music, and put out fresh scents. Use as many of your senses as you can when creating a relaxing atmosphere. See, hear, smell, and feel the relaxation all around you.
- *Get out into nature.* One way to unwind is to find a place in nature to spend some quiet time. This can be a walk or hike in the woods, reading in your favorite lounger in your backyard, or going to a local park. Being outside in

nature can be very refreshing and therapeutic. It is a reminder that life exists all around you on so many levels. While outside, take a few minutes just to be quiet and listen to the sounds all around you. Notice how many different sounds you can distinguish simultaneously. This exercise often puts your current circumstances into perspective with the grand scheme of things.

- *Read.* Many people read to unwind and relax. This is a wonderful idea, granted that the subject matter you are reading is relaxing and refreshing to you. When reading to relax, choose something that feels good to read.

- *Meditate or practice visualization.* This book has taught several forms of easy meditation and relaxation exercises. Meditation is any form of focused activity; visualization is imagery created by your brain to elicit a desired result. While these concepts are often misunderstood, they are simple and easy to use. As relaxation tools, they are quite beneficial. Use these techniques anytime you need them. They will help retrain your brain toward higher and brighter thinking.

- *Practice gratitude.* One way to relax and get in touch with yourself is to practice gratitude. Sit down for a gratitude session, and list (either on paper or in your mind) all the things in your life that you appreciate or are proud of. This is relaxing in that it enhances feelings of well-being to remember all the wonderful things that you have, every day, in your life.

- *Share with loved ones.* One way to relax is to spend time with those whom you love, in a comfortable and relaxing fashion. Gather for tea or coffee, go for a walk, or enjoy a nice, long phone conversation. Friends and loved ones enrich our lives and add beauty to our surroundings. Find time to appreciate them and share with them. You will be glad that you reconnected.

- *Pamper yourself.* There are countless ways to pamper yourself. You can buy yourself flowers, get a massage or manicure, treat yourself to a good movie, or take a mini-vacation. You can even do something as simple as allowing yourself five minutes of uninterrupted time to think and daydream. What you choose to do to pamper yourself is not nearly as important as the simple fact of doing something that makes you feel pampered. Do what is within your financial means and time frame, but do something just for you.

Tips for Staying Mentally Healthy

You can do many things inside your mind to create a better reality for your whole self. This is a brief reminder of ways in which you can monitor and improve your mental health.

- Monitor your thoughts and internal dialogues—think about what you think about.
- Begin to challenge these thoughts and hold them up to reality. Are you making mountains out of molehills? Do these thoughts serve you in some way? What are you gaining from thinking this way?
- Recognize what you can and cannot control. Accept that some things are just the way they are and cannot be changed, and learn how to change those things that you do have control over. Know when to take action and when to surrender.
- Change your thoughts to better serve you. They should be present-tense, positive, focused statements, or simple statements of fact.
- Think light. Find inspiration and motivation to work on your issues. Recognize that what you focus on becomes more real. Learn to create the reality that you want.

- Aim to do no harm. If you do no harm to others, you set the stage for others to do no harm to you. It doesn't always work out that way, but at least you're tilting the odds in your direction.
- Do not allow guilt or shame to plague you. If you can do something to alleviate your guilt and stop it from consuming your life, then do that. Get it over with and move on. Do penance and hope you've righted the wrong. If you haven't, you will get another chance. Be conscious of your current actions, but forgive yourself for your past ones. They are in the past. You cannot change them, but you can learn from them and move on.
- Forgive yourself. If you cannot forgive yourself, how do you expect others to forgive you?
- Find a way to let go of past hurts and forgive those who have harmed you. They were probably doing the best with what they had at the time (although this is not always the case, and is never an excuse for harmful behavior). Until and unless you have walked in another person's shoes, you cannot know what is really going on inside her mind. You don't know exactly what circumstances led to someone's behavior at a particular moment. Try to forgive just enough to ease the pain. Then, when you are ready, you can let it all go. You can release the grasp it has on you, and get it out of your life for a change.
- Pay attention to unexpected repetitions. If something happens repeatedly, there might be a message involved. Listen to your wise self. Know that your soul is there to help you. It cannot betray you. It is you.
- Learn your own personal coping style and use it. Relax when you need to relax. Take action when action is needed. Develop your own style of working through your problems in the best way for you.

Creating a New Reality

Now that you have considered these general techniques, let me show you how to actually create changes in your life. Here are three plans of action for specific circumstances in your life. From these three plans, you can create many more that are all your own. Remember, *you* are the expert on yourself. You know what you will and will not do. You know your strengths and weaknesses better than anyone. Commit to only those goals that you can see yourself reaching. If you do not believe you can accomplish something, then you will not accomplish it.

If these steps are not adequate for your circumstances, or you are unable to follow them on your own, you may need to seek outside help. You can call on a friend for support, or you can see a counselor or psychologist for assistance. Trust your inner judgment and listen to your inner messages. They will assist you on your way.

Plan of Action: Creating What You Desire

1. Set a goal, or determine what you would like to bring into your life.
2. Find congruence in your
   - thoughts, beliefs, and intentions;
   - behaviors, actions, and words; and
   - feelings and emotional states.
3. Clarify your goals and find better congruence.
   - What are the best thoughts you can have about this?
   - What are the best actions you can take?
   - What are the best feelings and attitudes you can maintain about this?
4. Decide on a course of action that feels good and right (upward and forward).

5. Do it.
6. Evaluate it.
   - If it doesn't work, modify it.
   - If something keeps repeating itself (a thought, feeling, etc.), examine it further to determine the reason for its persistence. Is there something you need to look at there?
   - Interrupt any patterns of dysfunction, with reevaluation and a new plan.
   - Apply continual modifications as necessary, until you create what you desire.

Plan of Action: Changing a Thought or Emotional State

When you catch yourself thinking unwanted thoughts or feeling unwanted emotions, use these techniques to change your emotional state.

1. Think about what is going on for a moment. Question this thought or feeling. Think it through.
2. Decide on a course of action that feels good and right (upward and forward). This most likely will include an alternate thought or belief that you can have, which will be more adaptive.
3. Do it. Think it. Replace the old thought with the new, more adaptive one.
4. Evaluate it.
   - If it doesn't work, modify it.
   - If the thought or feeling keeps coming back, examine it further to determine the reason for its persistence. Is there something you need to look at there?
   - Interrupt the pattern of dysfunction, with reevaluation and a new plan.

- Apply continual modifications as necessary to maintain optimal mental health.

Plan of Action: Creating a Better Personal Reality

I recommend getting a pen and paper for this exercise. Write down your answers after careful consideration. After careful self-analysis, figure out what feels good and right to you.

1. *Examine your current reality.* Look at your life, area by area: your relationships, your job, your home life, and the atmosphere in your mind. Is your life working? Are your thoughts adaptive? What is good in your life? What do you enjoy? Ask yourself these questions, and write down your responses.

   - Describe your current relationships with others. Focus on one or two main relationships, and describe your interactions, feelings, emotions, behaviors, level of respect or equality, level of sharing and caring, and any other aspect that may affect the way you feel and react.
   - Describe your work environment. How are your interactions with others at work? Do you feel valued? Is what you are doing beneficial to you or anyone else? Do you enjoy your work? What aspects of your work do you enjoy the most? What aspects of your job are not working? What could use improvement?
   - Describe your home life. Do you look forward to time at home? Do you enjoy the company of those you live with? Do you feel safe and secure while at home?
   - Describe the atmosphere in your mind. What are the main areas of concern? Do you worry too much? Are there areas you obsess over too frequently?

2. *Describe how you would like each area in your life to be.*

- Describe, on paper, how you would like your relationships to be. What types of interactions would you like to have with others? What types of feelings do you want to feel when you are around others?
- Describe how you would like things to be in your work environment. How would you like to be treated by others? What type of work would you like to do on a daily basis? What would you find fulfilling in your work?
- Describe how you would like your home life to be. How would you like everyone in your household to interact? How would you like to feel while you are at home? What activities would you like to do while at home?
- Describe how you would like the atmosphere in your mind to be. What do you want to think? How do you want to feel? How would you like to react to others?

3. *Prioritize.* Decide on an area you would like to work on first. Focus on something that is feasible to change. Begin with your thoughts when possible; once you are able to change your thoughts about something, everything else becomes easier.
4. *Make a plan of action.* Using the guidelines set in the previous examples, make a personal plan of action.
5. *Modify your plan when necessary.* Remember that life is not static. You continuously create and re-create your reality.

Know When to Get Outside Help

Knowing your boundaries and your limits is a vital aspect of your mental health. While you can do much work on your own, there are times and situations when you may need outside help. At these times, it is important for you to find an experienced therapist or doctor to help you. Look in your local yellow pages for the names of people in your area. Read their ads and get a feel for who they are. Check with your insurance carrier—they will have names of therapists in your area, and their credentials and areas of expertise. Determine if this person works hours when you can see them for sessions, and arrange a session when you are comfortable. Make sure to attend to your sessions and participate in *your* therapy. The therapist is not there for her mental health, she is there to help you find yours.

EPILOGUE

The only "real" way to live life is moment to moment, one experience at a time. You can learn to do this by becoming aware of the magnitude of each moment.

Appreciate your breathing and your body's ability to sustain life.
Taste your food.
Smell the roses.
Feel the warm cuddlies.
Hear the sweet sounds, and see the beauty of life all around you.
Use all your senses, all that you can.
Experience life.
Learn to love life.

Even if you love only certain aspects of life, you still love life. There is much to love if you are open to it. There is so much wonder and joy.

Your reality is what you, and those close to you, have created. You always have choices, and you are always held accountable for your actions. Only you can live your life. No one else can live it for you.

What are you waiting for?

Robin Klimpel McKnight, M.A., Licensed Professional Counselor, lives in the beautiful Pineywoods of East Texas with her husband, Jeremy, and son, William Bryson.

Robin has over ten years experience in the field of mental health. She has extensive experience in behavioral and cognitive behavioral therapy. She is certified in Critical Incident Stress Debriefing and has experience in private practice, public speaking, and mental health workshops. For contact information, please visit *www.creatingchange.info* or *www.robinmcknight.com*.

OTHER BOOKS FROM
BEYOND WORDS PUBLISHING, INC.

The Hidden Messages in Water
Author: Masaru Emoto
$16.95, softcover

Imagine if water could absorb feelings and emotions or be transformed by thoughts. Imagine if we could photograph the structure of water at the moment of freezing and from the image "read" a message about the water that is relevant to our own health and well-being on the planet. Imagine if we could show the direct consequences of destructive thoughts or, alternately, the thoughts of love and appreciation. *The Hidden Messages in Water* introduces readers to the revolutionary work of Japanese scientist Masaru Emoto, who discovered that molecules of water are affected by thoughts, words, and feelings. Dr. Emoto shares his realizations from his years of research and explains the profound implications on the healing of water, mankind, and earth.

Unclutter Your Life
Transforming Your Physical, Mental, and Emotional Space
Author: Katherine Gibson
$14.95, softcover

In this "run-and-grab" world, we stumble over the clutter that invades our homes and workplaces and assaults our minds and emotions. Clutter has us in a vice, and there's no letting go. Katherine Gibson exposes these obstacles for the self-stifling hindrances they are, including the guilt, self-doubt, envy, and toxic relationships that clutter the spirit. She offers tools to understand the physical and psychological chaos and confusion created by clutter and to create your own personal conclusions for restoring peace, harmony, and creativity in your life.

Ocean Oracle
What Seashells Reveal about Our True Nature
Author: Michelle Hanson
$26.95, boxed set (softcover with card deck)

Combining the ancient art of divination with the mysticism of seashells and their interaction with humankind throughout time, *Ocean Oracle: What Seashells Reveal about Our True Nature* borrows from many disciplines to produce a new and inspiring divination system based on seashells. The boxed set is comprised of 200 full-color seashell cards, a companion book, and a four-color foldout sheet with overview plates of the 200 shells. Appreciation for the shells' aesthetic beauty is enhanced by the text descriptions detailing the animals' behaviors, abilities, interactions with humankind, and their meaning. The shells serve as tools to assist you in revealing subconscious, hidden beliefs and attitudes.

The Truth about Beauty
Transforming Your Looks and Your Life from the Inside Out
Author: Kat James
$17.95, softcover

Nationally renowned holistic beauty expert and celebrity makeup artist Kat James presents a comprehensive health and beauty book that tells readers how to shed toxic and unnatural mind-sets and habits to let their real beauty shine through. Drawing from breaking science and her own remarkable metamorphosis, James offers lifestyle upgrades that can yield stunning physical rewards without drugs, surgery, sweat, or deprivation.

Beyond Stitch and Bitch
Reflections on Knitting and Life
$12.95, softcover

For those who knit, this book will remind you why you love this handicraft. Knitting is not only a craft but a hobby, a source of joy, a way to give, and a place to find peace. *Beyond Stitch and Bitch* is a collection of essays that explores the emotional and spiritual experiences common to those who knit. Its engaging, appealing stories chronicle how knitting can be a spiritual, meditative experience and how one can learn patience, creativity, discipline, and diligence from knitting. Intertwined with the essays are knitting patterns with easy how-to steps and photographs.

Path of the Pearl
Discover Your Treasures Within
Author: Mary Olsen Kelly
$16.95, hardcover

The pearl and its legendary mystical, restorative, and healing powers have ignited imaginations for centuries. *Path of the Pearl* captures the strength of this enduring symbol by using the pearl as a metaphor for personal growth. A pearl oyster, invaded by an irritant it can't expel, turns adversity into a glowing iridescent work of nature's art. This book acknowledges and celebrates the similar path shared by women, particularly in midlife.

The Power of Appreciation
The Key to a Vibrant Life
Authors: Noelle C. Nelson, Ph.D., and
Jeannine Lemare Calaba, Psy.D.
$14.95, softcover

Research confirms that when people feel appreciation, good things happen to their minds, hearts, and bodies. But appreciation is much more than a feel-good mantra. It is an actual force, an energy that can be harnessed and used to transform our daily life— relationships, work, health and aging, finances, crises, and more. *The Power of Appreciation* will open your eyes to the fabulous rewards of conscious, proactive appreciation. Based on a five-step approach to developing an appreciative mind-set, this handbook for living healthier and happier also includes tips for overcoming resistance and roadblocks, research supporting the positive effects of appreciation, and guidelines for creating an Appreciators Group.

To order or to request a catalog, contact
Beyond Words Publishing, Inc.
20827 N.W. Cornell Road, Suite 500
Hillsboro, OR 97124-9808
503-531-8700

You can also visit our Web site at *www.beyondword.com* or e-mail us at *info@beyondword.com*.

Beyond Words Publishing, Inc.

OUR CORPORATE MISSION

Inspire to Integrity

OUR DECLARED VALUES

We give to all of life as life has given us.
We honor all relationships.
Trust and stewardship are integral to fulfilling dreams.
Collaboration is essential to create miracles.
Creativity and aesthetics nourish the soul.
Unlimited thinking is fundamental.
Living your passion is vital.
Joy and humor open our hearts to growth.
It is important to remind ourselves of love.